DOVER · THRIFT · EDITIONS

Imagist Poetry
An Anthology

EDITED BY
BOB BLAISDELL

DOVER PUBLICATIONS, INC.
Mineola, New York

DOVER THRIFT EDITIONS

GENERAL EDITOR: PAUL NEGRI
EDITOR OF THIS VOLUME: BOB BLAISDELL

Copyright

Bibliographical Note

Imagist Poetry: An Anthology is a new work, first published by Dover Publications, Inc., in 1999.

Library of Congress Cataloging-in-Publication Data

Imagist poetry : an anthology / edited by Bob Blaisdell.
     p.   cm. — (Dover thrift editions)
  ISBN 0-486-40875-2 (pbk.)
   1. American poetry—20th century. 2. English poetry—20th century.
3. Imagist poetry. I. Blaisdell, Robert. II. Series.
PS613.I43 1999
811'.5208011—dc21
                                                99-25589
                                                 CIP

Manufactured in the United States of America
Dover Publications, Inc., 31 East 2nd Street, Mineola, N.Y. 11501

Note

"Why do we call ourselves 'Imagists'?" wrote Richard Aldington in 1914. "Well, why not? People say, 'Oh, because it looks silly, and everyone is some sort of an "ist," and why give yourselves a tag, and what on earth does it mean, and it's dam cheek any way.' Well, I think it a very good and descriptive title, and it serves to enunciate some of the principles we most firmly believe in." Among those principles, continued Aldington, were "1. Direct treatment of the subject . . . 2. As few adjectives as possible . . . 3. A hardness, as of cut stone . . . 4. Individuality of rhythm . . . 5. A whole lot of don'ts . . . 6. The exact word . . ."[1]

The Imagist movement of the 1910s extended the boundaries of twentieth-century poetry written in English. In 1913 the American Ezra Pound, only twenty-eight but already famous in London as an innovative poet and critic, published as an appendix to *Ripostes* (his latest book of verse), the philosopher T. E. Hulme's "collected poetry": five short, "imagistic" verses that illustrated the effectiveness of plain, direct language describing concrete particulars. With Aldington and H.D. (Hilda Doolittle), Pound recognized, publicized, and thereby primed and launched the Imagist movement. Pound and his American and British contemporaries' knowledge of French symbolist and impressionistic poetry and various classical literatures (Chinese, Japanese, and Greek, among others) allowed them to propound the unrealized and now obvious possibilities for poetry in English.

In 1914 Pound edited an anthology entitled *Des Imagistes*, which included his own poems as well as those by such relatively obscure young English and American writers as Aldington, H.D., F. S. Flint, and William Carlos Williams, in addition to the poetry of James Joyce and Ford Madox Hueffer. In spite of the disparagement and scoffing of some critics and established writers, greater and wider possibilities for

---

[1]"Modern Poetry and the Imagists," in *The Egoist* (London), June 1, 1914.

and conceptions of poetry in English suddenly came into play. In the controversy over the movement, Pound responded, "One 'discards rhyme,' not because one is incapable of rhyming neat, fleet, sweet, meet, treat, eat, feet, but because there are certain emotions or energies which are not to be represented by the over-familiar devices or patterns."[2] By the end of the decade, Imagism and its offspring or offshoots, including *vers libre*, were widely accepted by the reading public and experimented with by new and veteran poets.

Almost as soon as the movement was off the ground, Pound distanced himself from it, propounding instead Vorticism, a more personal interpretation and refinement of Imagism. He eventually dismissed the larger, less focused movement as "Amygisme," after Amy Lowell, an American patron of the arts and poet, who edited the next three Imagist anthologies, *Some Imagist Poets* (1915, 1916, 1917).

Some of the twentieth century's greatest poets in English, among them Pound, D. H. Lawrence, Wallace Stevens, Williams, H.D., and all of their literary descendants, owe much to Imagism, which, even when metamorphosed, idiosyncratically applied, abandoned, or renounced, created a larger playing field for the game of poetry.

Many of the poems included in this selection appeared first in the *Des Imagistes* and *Some Imagist Poets* anthologies; others appeared in contemporary journals (most notably *Poetry, The Dial, The Trend,* and *The Egoist*) and in books by the represented poets. The basis for inclusion in this edition's selection of the thousands of "imagistic" verses between 1913 and 1922 lies in their strengths as individual poems and as characteristic illustrations of Imagism.

---

[2]"Affirmations: As for Imagisme," in *The New Age*, January 28, 1915.

Contents

RICHARD ALDINGTON
(1892–1962)

The Poplar

Why do you always stand there shivering
Between the white stream and the road?

The people pass through the dust
On bicycles, in carts, in motor-cars;
The waggoners go by at dawn;
The lovers walk on the grass path at night.

Stir from your roots, walk, poplar!
You are more beautiful than they are.

I know that the white wind loves you,
Is always kissing you and turning up
The white lining of your green petticoat.
The sky darts through you like blue rain,
And the grey rain drips on your flanks
And loves you.
And I have seen the moon
Slip his silver penny into your pocket
As you straightened your hair;
And the white mist curling and hesitating
Like a bashful lover about your knees.

I know you, poplar;
I have watched you since I was ten.
But if you had a little real love,
A little strength,
You would leave your nonchalant idle lovers
And go walking down the white road
Behind the waggoners.

1

There are beautiful beeches down beyond the hill.
Will you always stand there shivering?

Summer

A butterfly,
Black and scarlet,
Spotted with white,
Fans its wings
Over a privet flower.

A thousand crimson foxgloves,
Tall bloody pikes,
Stand motionless in the gravel quarry;
The wind runs over them.

A rose film over a pale sky
Fantastically cut by dark chimneys;
Candles winking in the windows
Across an old city-garden.

Evening

The chimneys, rank on rank,
Cut the clear sky;
The moon
With a rag of gauze about her loins
Poses among them, an awkward Venus—

And here am I looking wantonly at her
Over the kitchen sink.

Choricos

The ancient songs
Pass deathward mournfully.

Cold lips that sing no more, and withered wreaths,
Regretful eyes, and drooping breasts and wings—

Symbols of ancient songs
Mournfully passing
Down to the great white surges,
Watched of none
Save the frail sea-birds
And the lithe pale girls,
Daughters of Okeanus.

And the songs pass
From the green land
Which lies upon the waves as a leaf
On the flowers of hyacinth;
And they pass from the waters,
The manifold winds and the dim moon,
And they come,
Silently winging through soft Kimmerian dusk,
To the quiet level lands
That she keeps for us all,
That she wrought for us all for sleep
In the silver days of the earth's dawning—
Proserpina, daughter of Zeus.

And we turn from the Kuprian's breasts,
And we turn from thee,
Phoibos Apollon,
And we turn from the music of old
And the hills that we loved and the meads,
And we turn from the fiery day,
And the lips that were over sweet;
For silently
Brushing the fields with red-shod feet,
With purple robe
Searing the flowers as with a sudden flame,
Death,
Thou hast come upon us.

And of all the ancient songs
Passing to the swallow-blue halls
By the dark streams of Persephone,
This only remains:
That we turn to thee,
Death,
That we turn to thee, singing
One last song.

O Death,
Thou art an healing wind
That blowest over white flowers
A-tremble with dew;
Thou art a wind flowing
Over dark leagues of lonely sea;
Thou art the dusk and the fragrance;
Thou art the lips of love mournfully smiling;
Thou art the pale peace of one
Satiate with old desires;
Thou art the silence of beauty,
And we look no more for the morning
We yearn no more for the sun,
Since with thy white hands,
Death,
Thou crownest us with the pallid chaplets,
The slim colourless poppies
Which in thy garden alone
Softly thou gatherest.

And silently,
And with slow feet approaching,
And with bowed head and unlit eyes,
We kneel before thee:
And thou, leaning towards us,
Caressingly layest upon us
Flowers from thy thin cold hands,
And, smiling as a chaste woman
Knowing love in her heart,
Thou sealest our eyes
And the illimitable quietude
Comes gently upon us.

To a Greek Marble

Πότνια, πότνια[1]
White grave goddess,
Pity my sadness,
O silence of Paros.

---

[1]Πότνια, πότνια] O goddess, O goddess

I am not of these about thy feet,
These garments and decorum;
I am thy brother,
Thy lover of aforetime crying to thee,
And thou hearest me not.

I have whispered thee in thy solitudes
Of our loves in Phrygia,
The far ecstasy of burning noons
When the fragile pipes
Ceased in the cypress shade,
And the brown fingers of the shepherd
Moved over slim shoulders;
And only the cicada sang.

I have told thee of the hills
And the lisp of reeds
And the sun upon thy breasts,

And thou hearest me not,
Πότνια, πότνια
Thou hearest me not.

Au Vieux Jardin

I have sat here happy in the gardens,
Watching the still pool and the reeds
And the dark clouds
Which the wind of the upper air
Tore like the green leafy boughs
Of the divers-hued trees of late summer;
But though I greatly delight
In these and the water lilies,
That which sets me nighest to weeping
Is the rose and white colour of the smooth flag-stones,
And the pale yellow grasses
Among them.

Lesbia

Use no more speech now;
Let the silence spread gold hair above us
Fold on delicate fold;
You had the ivory of my life to carve.
Use no more speech.

*   *   *   *

And Picus of Mirandola is dead;
And all the gods they dreamed and fabled of,
Hermes, and Thoth, and Christ, are rotten now,
Rotten and dank.

*   *   *   *

And through it all I see your pale Greek face;
Tenderness makes me as eager as a little child
To love you

You morsel left half cold on Caesar's plate.

Beauty Thou Hast Hurt Me Overmuch

The light is a wound to me.
The soft notes
Feed upon the wound.

Where wert thou born
O thou woe
That consumest my life?
Whither comest thou?

Toothed wind of the seas,
No man knows thy beginning.
As a bird with strong claws
Thou woundest me,
O beautiful sorrow.

Argyria

O you,
O you most fair,
Swayer of reeds, whisperer
Among the flowering rushes,
You have hidden your hands
Beneath the poplar leaves,
You have given them to the white waters.

Swallow-fleet,
Sea-child cold from waves,
Slight reed that sang so blithely in the wind,
White cloud the white sun kissed into the air;
Pan mourns for you.

White limbs, white song,
Pan mourns for you.

In the Via Sestina

O daughter of Isis,
Thou standest beside the wet highway
Of this decayed Rome,
A manifest harlot.

Straight and slim art thou
As a marble phallus;
Thy face is the face of Isis
Carven

As she is carven in basalt.
And my heart stops with awe
At the presence of the gods,

There beside thee on the stall of images
Is the head of Osiris
Thy lord.

The River

I

I drifted along the river
Until I moored my boat
By these crossed trunks.

Here the mist moves
Over fragile leaves and rushes,
Colourless waters and brown fading hills.

She has come from beneath the trees,
Moving within the mist,
A floating leaf.

II

O blue flower of the evening,
You have touched my face
With your leaves of silver.

Love me for I must depart.

Bromios

The withered bonds are broken.
The waxed reeds and the double pipe
Clamour about me;
The hot wind swirls
Through the red pine trunks.

Io! the fauns and the satyrs.
The touch of their shagged curled fur
And blunt horns!

They have wine in heavy craters
Painted black and red;
Wine to splash on her white body.
Io!
She shrinks from the cold shower—
Afraid, afraid!

Let the Maenads break through the myrtles
And the boughs of the rohododaphnai.

Let them tear the quick deers' flesh.
Ah, the cruel, exquisite fingers!

Io!
I have brought you the brown clusters,
The ivy-boughs and pine-cones.

Your breasts are cold sea-ripples,
But they smell of the warm grasses.

Throw wide the chiton and the peplum,
Maidens of the Dew.
Beautiful are your bodies, O Maenads,
Beautiful the sudden folds,
The vanishing curves of the white linen
About you.

Io!
Hear the rich laughter of the forest,
The cymbals,
The trampling of the panisks and the centaurs.

To Atthis

(After the Manuscript of Sappho now in Berlin)

Atthis, far from me and dear Mnasidika,
Dwells in Sardis;
Many times she was near us
So that we lived life well
Like the far-famed goddess
Whom above all things music delighted.

And now she is first among the Lydian women
As the mighty sun, the rose-fingered moon,
Beside the great stars.

And the light fades from the bitter sea
And in like manner from the rich-blossoming earth;
And the dew is shed upon the flowers,
Rose and soft meadow-sweet
And many-coloured melilote.

Many things told are remembered of sterile Atthis.

I yearn to behold thy delicate soul
To satiate my desire. . . .
. . . .

The Faun Sees Snow for the First Time

Zeus,
Brazen-thunder-hurler,
Cloud-whirler, son-of-Kronos,
Send vengeance on these Oreads
Who strew
White frozen flecks of mist and cloud
Over the brown trees and the tufted grass
Of the meadows, where the stream
Runs black through shining banks
Of bluish white.

Zeus,
Are the halls of heaven broken up
That you flake down upon me
Feather-strips of marble?

Dis and Styx!
When I stamp my hoof
The frozen-cloud-specks jam into the cleft
So that I reel upon two slippery points. . . .

Fool, to stand here cursing
When I might be running!

At the British Museum

I turn the page and read:
"I dream of silent verses where the rhyme
Glides noiseless as an oar."

The heavy musty air, the black desks,
The bent heads and the rustling noises
In the great dome
Vanish. . . .
And

The sun hangs in the cobalt-blue sky,
The boat drifts over the lake shallows,
The fishes skim like umber shades through the undulating weeds,
The oleanders drop their rosy petals on the lawns,
And the swallows dive and swirl and whistle
About the cleft battlements of Can Grande's castle. . . .

Images

I

Like a gondola of green scented fruits
Drifting along the dark canals of Venice,
You, O exquisite one,
Have entered into my desolate city.

II

The blue smoke leaps
Like swirling clouds of birds vanishing,
So my love leaps forth towards you,
Vanishes and is renewed.

III

A rose-yellow moon in a pale sky
When the sunset is faint vermilion
In the mist among the tree-boughs
Art thou to me, my beloved.

IV

A young beech tree on the edge of the forest
Stands still in the evening,
Yet shudders through all its leaves in the light air
And seems to fear the stars—
So are you still and so tremble.

V

The red deer are high on the mountain,
They are beyond the last pine-trees,
And my desires have run with them.

VI

The flower which the wind has shaken
Is soon filled again with rain;
So does my heart fill slowly with tears
Until you return.

Amalfi

We will come down to you,
O very deep sea,
And drift upon your pale green waves
Like scattered petals.

We will come down to you from the hills,
From the scented lemon-groves,
From the hot sun.
We will come down,
O Thalassa,
And drift upon
Your pale green waves
Like petals.

At Nights

At nights I sit here,
Shading my eyes, shutting them if you glance up,
Pretending to doze,
And watching you,
Thinking . . .

I think of when I first saw the beauty of things—
God knows I was poor enough and sad enough
And humiliated enough—
But not all the slights and the poorness and the worry
Could hide away the green of the poplar leaves,
The ripples and light of the little stream,
The pattern of the ducks' feathers—
Like a Japanese print—
The dawns I saw in the winter

When I went shooting,
The summer walks and the winter walks,
The hot days with the cows coming down to the water,
The flowers,
Buttercups, meadowsweet, hog's parsley,
And the larks singing in the morning
And the thrushes singing at evening
When I went out in the fields, muttering poetry . . .

I looked at the world as God did
When first He made it.
I saw that it was good.

And now at nights,
Now that everything has gone right somehow,
And I have friends and books
And no more bitterness,
I sit here, shading my eyes,
Peeping at you, watching you,
Thinking.

London

(May, 1915)

Glittering leaves
Dance in a squall;
Behind them bleak immoveable clouds.

A church spire
Holds up a little brass cock
To peck at the blue wheatfields.

Roofs, conical spires, tapering chimneys,
Livid with sunlight, lace the horizon.

A pear-tree, a broken white pyramid
In a dingy garden, troubles me
With ecstasy.

At night, the moon, a pregnant woman
Walks cautiously over the slippery heavens.

And I am tormented,
Obsessed,

Among all this beauty,
With a vision of ruins,
Of walls crumbling into clay.

Images

I

Through the dark pine trunks
Silver and yellow gleam the clouds
And the sun;
The sea is faint purple.
My love, my love, I shall never reach you.

II

You are beautiful
As a straight red fox-glove
Among green plants;
I stretched out my hand to caress you:
It is blistered by the envious nettles.

III

I have spent hours this morning
Seeking in the brook
For a clear pebble
To remind me of your eyes.

And all the sleepless hours of night
I think of you.

IV

Your kisses are poignant,
Ah! why must I leave you?

Here alone I scribble and re-scribble
The words of a long-dead Greek poet:
"Love, thou art terrible,
Ah, Love, thou art bitter-sweet!"

Insouciance

In and out of the dreary trenches,
Trudging cheerily under the stars,
I make for myself little poems
Delicate as a flock of doves.

They fly away like white-winged doves.

Two Impressions

I

The colorless morning glides upward
Over the marsh and ragged trees.

Though our mood be sombre
And our bodies angry for more sleep,
This feathered softness of pale light,
Falling negligently upon us,
Delights us.

II

High above the drab barren ground
Three herons beat across the dawn-blue sky.
They drift slowly away
Until they appear
As three horizontal umber brush-strokes
On finely shaded cobalt.
And the mist, driven by the wind
Up and across the distant hill,
Gleams like soft white hair
Brushed amorously backward!

WALTER CONRAD ARENSBERG
(1878–1954)

Voyage à l'Infini

The swan existing
Is like a song with an accompaniment
Imaginary.

Across the grassy lake,
Across the lake to the shadow of the willows,
It is accompanied by an image—
As by Debussy's
"Reflets dans l'eau."

The swan that is
Reflects
Upon the solitary water—breast to breast
With the duplicity:
"The other one!"

And breast to breast it is confused.
O visionary wedding! O stateliness of the procession!
It is accompanied by the image of itself
Alone.

At night
The lake is a wide silence,
Without imagination.

SKIPWITH CANNÉLL
(1887–1957)

Nocturnes

I

Thy feet,
That are like little, silver birds,
Thou hast set upon pleasant ways;
Therefore I will follow thee,
Thou Dove of the Golden Eyes,
Upon any path will I follow thee,
For the light of thy beauty
Shines before me like a torch.

II

Thy feet are white
Upon the foam of the sea;
Hold me fast, thou bright Swan,
Lest I stumble,
And into deep waters.

III

Long have I been
But the Singer beneath thy Casement,
And now I am weary.
I am sick with longing,
O my Belovéd;
Therefore bear me with thee
Swiftly
Upon our road.

IV

With the net of thy hair
Thou hast fished in the sea,
And a strange fish
Hast thou caught in thy net;
For thy hair,
Belovéd,
Holdeth my heart
Within its web of gold.

V

I am weary with love, and thy lips
Are night-born poppies.
Give me therefore thy lips
That I may know sleep.

VI

I am weary with longing,
I am faint with love;
For upon my head has the moonlight
Fallen
As a sword.

ADELAIDE CRAPSEY
(1878–1914)

November Night

Listen . . .
With faint dry sound,
Like steps of passing ghosts,
The leaves, frost-crisp'd, break from the trees
And fall.

The Guarded Wound

If it
Were lighter touch
Than petal of flower resting
On grass, oh still too heavy it were,
Too heavy!

The Warning

Just now,
Out of the strange
Still dusk . . . as strange, as still . . .
A white moth flew. Why am I grown
So cold?

Niagara

Seen on a Night in November

How frail
Above the bulk
Of crashing water hangs,
Autumnal, evanescent, wan,
The moon.

On Seeing Weather-Beaten Trees

Is it as plainly in our living shown,
By slant and twist, which way the wind hath blown?

Old Love

More dim than waning moon
Thy face, more faint
Than is the falling wind
Thy voice, yet do
Thine eyes most strangely glow,
Thou ghost . . . thou ghost.

Night

I have minded me
Of the noon-day brightness,
And the crickets' drowsy
Singing in the sunshine . . .

I have minded me
Of the slim marsh-grasses
That the winds at twilight,
Dying, scarcely ripple . . .

And I cannot sleep.

I have minded me
Of a lily-pond,
Where the waters sway
All the moonlit leaves
And the curled long stems . . .

And I cannot sleep.

H.D. [HILDA DOOLITTLE]
(1886–1961)

Sitalkas

Thou art come at length
More beautiful
Than any cool god
In a chamber under
Lycia's far coast,
Than any high god
Who touches us not
Here in the seeded grass.
Aye, than Argestes
Scattering the broken leaves.

Hermes of the Ways

I

The hard sand breaks,
And the grains of it
Are clear as wine.

Far off over the leagues of it,
The wind,
Playing on the wide shore,
Piles little ridges,
And the great waves
Break over it.

But more than the many-foamed ways
Of the sea,
I know him
Of the triple path-ways,
Hermes,
Who awaiteth.

Dubious,
Facing three ways,
Welcoming wayfarers,
He whom the sea-orchard
Shelters from the west,
From the east
Weathers sea-wind;
Fronts the great dunes.

Wind rushes
Over the dunes,
And the coarse, salt-crusted grass
Answers.

Heu,
It whips round my ankles!

II

Small is
This white stream,
Flowing below ground
From the poplar-shaded hill,
But the water is sweet.

Apples on the small trees
Are hard,
Too small,
Too late ripened
By a desperate sun
That struggles through sea-mist.

The boughs of the trees
Are twisted
By many bafflings;
Twisted are
The small-leafed boughs.
But the shadow of them

Is not the shadow of the mast head
Nor of the torn sails.

Hermes, Hermes,
The great sea foamed,
Gnashed its teeth about me;
But you have waited,
Where sea-grass tangles with
Shore-grass.

Priapus

Keeper-of-Orchards

I saw the first pear
As it fell.
The honey-seeking, golden-banded,
The yellow swarm
Was not more fleet than I,
(Spare us from loveliness!)
And I fell prostrate,
Crying,
Thou hast flayed us with thy blossoms;
Spare us the beauty
Of fruit-trees!

The honey-seeking
Paused not,
The air thundered their song,
And I alone was prostrate.

O rough-hewn
God of the orchard,
I bring thee an offering;
Do thou, alone unbeautiful
(Son of the god),
Spare us from loveliness.

The fallen hazel-nuts,
Stripped late of their green sheaths,
The grapes, red-purple,
Their berries
Dripping with wine,
Pomegranates already broken,

And shrunken fig,
And quinces untouched,
I bring thee as offering.

Acon

(After Joannes Baptista Amaltheus)

I

Bear me to Dictaeus,
And to the steep slopes;
To the river Erymanthus.

I choose spray of dittany,
Cyperum frail of flower,
Buds of myrrh,
All-healing herbs,
Close pressed in calathes.

For she lies panting,
Drawing sharp breath,
Broken with harsh sobs,
She, Hyella,
Whom no god pitieth.

II

Dryads,
Haunting the groves,
Nereids,
Who dwell in wet caves,
For all the whitish leaves of olive-branch,
And early roses,
And ivy wreathes, woven gold berries,
Which she once brought to your altars,
Bear now ripe fruits from Arcadia,
And Assyrian wine
To shatter her fever.

The light of her face falls from its flower,
As a hyacinth,
Hidden in a far valley,
Perishes upon burnt grass.

Pales,
Bring gifts,
Bring your Phoenician stuffs,
And do you, fleet-footed nymphs,
Bring offerings,
Illyrian iris,
And a branch of shrub,
And frail-headed poppies.

Hermonax

Gods of the sea;
Ino,
Leaving warm meads
For the green, grey-green fastnesses
Of the great deeps;
And Palemon,
Bright striker of sea-shaft,
Hear me.

Let all whom the sea loveth,
Come to its altar front,
And I
Who can offer no other sacrifice to thee
Bring this.

Broken by great waves,
The wavelets flung it here,
This sea-gliding creature,
This strange creature like a weed,
Covered with salt foam,
Torn from the hillocks
Of rock.

I, Hermonax,
Caster of nets,
Risking chance,
Plying the sea craft,
Came on it.

Thus to sea god
Cometh gift of sea wrack;
I, Hermonax, offer it

To thee, Ino,
And to Palemon.

Epigram

(After the Greek)

The golden one is gone from the banquets;
She, beloved of Atimetus,
The swallow, the bright Homonoea:
Gone the dear chatterer.

The Pool

Are you alive?
I touch you.
You quiver like a sea-fish.
I cover you with my net.
What are you—banded one?

The Garden

I

You are clear,
O rose, cut in rock,
hard as the descent of hail.

I could scrape the colour
from the petal,
like spilt dye from a rock.

If I could break you
I could break a tree.

If I could stir
I could break a tree,
I could break you.

II

O wind,
rend open the heat,
cut apart the heat,
rend it sideways.

Fruit can not drop
through this thick air:
fruit can not fall into heat
that presses up and blunts
the points of pears
and rounds the grapes.

Cut the heat,
plough through it,
turning it on either side
of your path.

Oread

Whirl up, sea—
Whirl your pointed pines,
Splash your great pines
On our rocks,
Hurl your green over us,
Cover us with your pools of fir.

Mid-Day

The light beats upon me.
I am startled—
A split leaf crackles on the paved floor—
I am anguished—defeated.

A slight wind shakes the seed-pods.
My thoughts are spent
As the black seeds.
My thoughts tear me.
I dread their fever—
I am scattered in its whirl.

I am scattered like
The hot shrivelled seeds.

The shrivelled seeds
Are spilt on the path.
The grass bends with dust.
The grape slips
Under its crackled leaf:
Yet far beyond the spent seed-pods,
And the blackened stalks of mint,
The poplar is bright on the hill,
The poplar spreads out,
Deep-rooted among trees.

O poplar, you are great
Among the hill-stones,
While I perish on the path
Among the crevices of the rocks.

Eurydice

I

So you have swept me back—
I who could have walked with the live souls
above the earth,
I who could have slept among the live flowers
at last.

So for your arrogance
and your ruthlessness
I am swept back
where dead lichens drip
dead cinders upon moss of ash.

So for your arrogance
I am broken at last,
I who had lived unconscious,
who was almost forgot.

If you had let me wait
I had grown from listlessness
into peace—
if you had let me rest with the dead,

I had forgot you
and the past.

II

Here only flame upon flame
and black among the red sparks,
streaks of black and light
grown colourless.

Why did you turn back,
that hell should be reinhabited
of myself thus
swept into nothingness?

Why did you turn,
why did you glance back—
why did you hesitate for that moment,
why did you bend your face
caught with the flame of the upper earth
above my face?

What was it that crossed my face
with the light from yours
and your glance?

What was it you saw in my face—
the light of your own face,
the fire of your own presence?

What had my face to offer
but reflex of the earth—
hyacinth colour
caught from the raw fissure in the rock
where the light struck,
and the colour of azure crocuses
and the bright surface of gold crocuses
and of the wind-flower,
swift in its veins as lightning
and as white.

III

Saffron from the fringe of the earth,
wild saffron that has bent
over the sharp edge of earth,
all the flowers that cut through the earth,

all, all the flowers are lost.

Everything is lost,
everything is crossed with black,
black upon black
and worse than black—
this colourless light.

IV

Fringe upon fringe
of blue crocuses,
crocuses, walled against blue of themselves,
blue of that upper earth,
blue of the depth upon depth of flowers—
lost!

Flowers—
if I could have taken once my breath of them,
enough of them,
more than earth,
even than of the upper earth,
had passed with me
beneath the earth!

If I could have caught up from the earth,
the whole of the flowers of the earth,
if once I could have breathed into myself
the very golden crocuses
and the red,
and the very golden hearts of the first saffron,
the whole of the golden mass,
the whole of the great fragrance,
I could have dared the loss.

V

So for your arrogance
and your ruthlessness
I have lost the earth
and the flowers of the earth,
and the live souls above the earth,

and you who passed across the light
and reached
ruthless—

you who have your own light,
who are to yourself a presence,
who need no presence.

Yet for all your arrogance
and your glance,
I tell you this—
such loss is no loss,
such terror, such coils and strands and pitfalls
of blackness,
such terror
is no loss.

Hell is no worse than your earth
above the earth,
hell is no worse—
no—nor your flowers
nor your veins of light
nor your presence,
a loss.

My hell is no worse than yours
though you pass among the flowers and speak
with the spirits above earth.

VI

Against the black
I have more fervour
than you in all the splendour of that place,
against the blackness
and the stark grey
I have more light!

And the flowers—
if I should tell you,
you would turn from your own fit paths
toward hell—
turn again and glance back

and I would sink into a place
even more terrible than this.

VII

At least I have the flowers of myself
and my thoughts—no god

can take that!
I have the fervour of myself for a presence
and my own spirit for light.

And my spirit with its loss
knows this:
though small against the black,
small against the formless rocks,
hell must break before I am lost.

Before I am lost,
hell must open like a red rose
for the dead to pass.

Fragment XXXVI

I know not what to do:
My mind is divided.
*   —Sappho*

I know not what to do—
My mind is reft.
Is song's gift best?
Is love's gift loveliest?
I know not what to do,
Now sleep has pressed
Weight on your eyelids.

Shall I break your rest,
Devouring, eager?
Is love's gift best?—
Nay, song's the loveliest.
Yet, were you lost,
What rapture could I take from song?—
What song were left?

I know not what to do:
To turn and slake
The rage that burns,
With my breath burn
And trouble your cool breath—
So shall I turn and take
Snow in my arms,
(Is love's gift best?)

Yet flake on flake
Of snow were comfortless,
Did you lie wondering,
Wakened yet unawake.

Shall I turn and take
Comfortless snow within my arms,
Press lips to lips that answer not,
Press lips to flesh
That shudders not nor breaks?

Is love's gift best?—
Shall I turn and slake
All the wild longing?
Oh, I am eager for you!
As the Pleiads shake
White light in whiter water,
So shall I take you?

My mind is quite divided;
My minds hesitate,
So perfect matched
I know not what to do.
Each strives with each:
As two white wrestlers,
Standing for a match,
Ready to turn and clutch,
Yet never shake
Muscle or nerve or tendon;
So my mind waits
To grapple with my mind—
Yet I am quiet,
I would seem at rest.

I know not what to do.
Strain upon strain,
Sound surging upon sound,
Makes my brain blind;
As a wave line may wait to fall,
Yet waiting for its falling
Still the wind may take,
From off its crest,
White flake on flake of foam,
That rises
Seeming to dart and pulse

And rend the light,
So my mind hesitates
Above the passion
Quivering yet to break,
So my mind hesitates above my mind
Listening to song's delight.

I know not what to do.
Will the sound break,
Rending the night
With rift on rift of rose
And scattered light?
Will the sound break at last
As the wave hesitant,
Or will the whole night pass
And I lie listening awake?

Song

You are as gold
As the half-ripe grain
That merges to gold again,
As white as the white rain
That beats through
The half-opened flowers
Of the great flower tufts
Thick on the black limbs
Of an Illyrian apple bough.

Can honey distil such fragrance
As your bright hair?—
For your face is as fair as rain,
Yet as rain that lies clear
On white honey-comb
Lends radiance to the white wax,
So your hair on your brow
Casts light for a shadow.

At Baia

I should have thought
In a dream you would have brought
Some lovely perilous thing:
Orchids piled in a great sheath,
As who would say, in a dream,
"I send you this,
Who left the blue veins
Of your throat unkissed."

Why was it that your hands,
That never took mine—
Your hands that I could see
Drift over the orchid heads
So carefully;
Your hands, so fragile, sure to lift
So gently, the fragile flower stuff—
Ah, ah, how was it

You never sent, in a dream,
The very form, the very scent,
Not heavy, not sensuous,
But perilous—perilous!—
Of orchids, piled in a great sheath,
And folded underneath on a bright scroll,
Some word:

Flower sent to flower;
For white hands the lesser white,
Less lovely, of flower leaf.

Or,

Lover to lover—no kiss,
No touch, but forever and ever this!

JOHN GOULD FLETCHER
(1886–1950)

Irradiations

I

Over the roof-tops race the shadows of clouds:
Like horses the shadows of clouds charge down the street.

Whirlpools of purple and gold,
Winds from the mountains of cinnabar,
Lacquered mandarin moments, palanquins swaying and balancing
Amid the vermilion pavilions, against the jade balustrades;
Glint of the glittering wings of dragon-flies in the light;
Silver filaments, golden flakes settling downwards;
Rippling, quivering flutters; repulse and surrender,
The sun broidered upon the rain,
The rain rustling with the sun.

Over the roof-tops race the shadows of clouds:
Like horses the shadows of clouds charge down the street.

II

O seeded grass, you army of little men
Crawling up the low slopes with quivering quick blades of steel:
You who storm millions of graves, tiny green tentacles of earth,
Interlace your tangled webs tightly over my heart
And do not let me go:
For I would lie here for ever and watch with one eye
The pilgrimaging ants in your dull savage jungles,
While with the other I see the long lines of the slope
Break in mid air, a wave surprisingly arrested;
And above it, wavering, bodiless, colorless, unreal,
The long thin lazy fingers of the heat.

III

Not noisily, but solemnly and pale,
In a meditative ecstasy, you entered life,
As for some strange rite, to which you alone held the clue.
Child, life did not give rude strength to you;
From the beginning you would seem to have thrown away,
As something cold and cumbersome, that armor men use against
    death.
You would perchance look on death face to face and from him wrest
    the secret
Whether his face wears oftenest a smile or no?
Strange, old and silent being, there is something
Infinitely vast in your intense tininess:
I think you could point out with a smile some curious star
Far off in the heavens which no man has seen before.

IV

The morning is clean and blue, and the wind blows up the clouds:
Now my thoughts, gathered from afar,
Once again in their patched armor, with rusty plumes and blunted
    swords,
Move out to war.

Smoking our morning pipes we shall ride two and two
Through the woods.
For our old cause keeps us together,
And our hatred is so precious not death or defeat can break it.

God willing, we shall this day meet that old enemy
Who has given us so many a good beating.
Thank God, we have a cause worth fighting for,
And a cause worth losing, and a good song to sing!

*   *   *   *

X

The trees, like great jade elephants,
Chained, stamp and shake 'neath the gadflies of the breeze;
The trees lunge and plunge, unruly elephants:
The clouds are their crimson howdah-canopies,
The sunlight glints like the golden robe of a Shah.
Would I were tossed on the wrinkled backs of these trees.

The Windmills

The windmills, like great sunflowers of steel,
Lift themselves proudly over the straggling houses;
And at their feet the deep blue-green alfalfa
Cuts the desert like the stroke of a sword.

Yellow melon flowers
Crawl beneath the withered peach-trees;
A date-palm throws its heavy fronds of steel
Against the scoured metallic sky.

The houses, doubled-roofed for coolness,
Cower amid the manzanita scrub.
A man with jingling spurs
Walks heavily out of a vine-bowered doorway,
Mounts his pony, rides away.

The windmills stare at the sun.
The yellow earth cracks and blisters.
Everything is still.

In the afternoon
The wind takes dry waves of heat and tosses them,
Mingled with dust, up and down the streets,
Against the belfry with its green bells:

And, after sunset, when the sky
Becomes a green and orange fan,
The windmills, like great sunflowers on dried stalks,
Stare hard at the sun they cannot follow.

Turning, turning, forever turning
In the chill night-wind that sweeps over the valley,
With the shriek and the clank of the pumps groaning beneath them,
And the choking gurgle of tepid water.

Mexican Quarter

By an alley lined with tumble-down shacks
And street-lamps askew, half-sputtering,
Feebly glimmering on gutters choked with filth and dogs
Scratching their mangy backs:

Half-naked children are running about,
Women puff cigarettes in black doorways,
Crickets are crying.
Men slouch sullenly
Into the shadows:
Behind a hedge of cactus,
The smell of a dead horse
Mingles with the smell of tamales frying.

And a girl in a black lace shawl
Sits in a rickety chair by the square of an unglazed window,
And sees the explosion of the stars
Softly poised on a velvet sky.
And she is humming to herself:—
"Stars, if I could reach you,
(You are so very clear that it seems as if I could reach you)
I would give you all to Madonna's image,
On the grey-plastered altar behind the paper flowers,
So that Juan would come back to me,
And we could live again those lazy burning hours
Forgetting the tap of my fan and my sharp words.
And I would only keep four of you,
Those two blue-white ones overhead,
To hang in my ears;
And those two orange ones yonder,
To fasten on my shoe-buckles."

A little further along the street
A man sits stringing a brown guitar.
The smoke of his cigarette curls round his head,
And he, too, is humming, but other words:
"Think not that at your window I wait;
New love is better, the old is turned to hate.
Fate! Fate! All things pass away;
Life is forever, youth is for a day.
Love again if you may
Before the stars are blown out of the sky
And the crickets die;
Babylon and Samarkand
Are mud walls in a waste of sand."

Rain in the Desert

The huge red-buttressed mesa over yonder
Is merely a far-off temple where the sleepy sun is burning
Its altar-fires of pinyon and of toyon for the day.

The old priests sleep, white-shrouded,
Their pottery whistles lie beside them, the prayer-sticks closely
    feathered;
On every mummied face there glows a smile.

The sun is rolling slowly
Beneath the sluggish folds of the sky-serpents,
Coiling, uncoiling, blue-black, sparked with fires.

The old dead priests
Feel in the thin dried earth that is heaped about them,
Above the smell of scorching oozing pinyon,
The acrid smell of rain.

And now the showers
Surround the mesa like a troop of silver dancers:
Shaking their rattles, stamping, chanting, roaring,
Whirling, extinguishing the last red wisp of light.

Clouds Across the Canyon

Shadows of clouds
March across the canyon,
Shadows of blue hands passing
Over a curtain of flame.

Clutching, staggering, upstriking,
Darting in blue-black fury,
To where pinnacles, green and orange,
Await.

The winds are battling and striving to break them:
Thin lightnings spit and flicker,
The peaks seem a dance of scarlet demons
Flitting amid the shadows.

Grey rain-curtains wave afar off,
Wisps of vapour curl and vanish.
The sun throws soft shafts of golden light
Over rose-buttressed palisades.

Now the clouds are a lazy procession;
Blue balloons bobbing solemnly
Over black-dappled walls,

Where rise sharp-fretted, golden-roofed cathedrals
Exultantly, and split the sky with light.

The Skaters

To A. D. R.

Black swallows swooping or gliding
In a flurry of entangled loops and curves;
The skaters skim over the frozen river.
And the grinding click of their skates as they impinge upon the
    surface,
Is like the brushing together of thin wing-tips of silver.

F. S. FLINT
(1885–1960)

"London, my beautiful"

London, my beautiful,
it is not the sunset
nor the pale green sky
shimmering through the curtain
of the silver birch,
nor the quietness;
it is not the hopping
of birds
upon the lawn,
nor the darkness
stealing over all things
that moves me.

But as the moon creeps slowly
over the tree-tops
among the stars,
I think of her
and the glow her passing
sheds on men.

London, my beautiful,
I will climb
into the branches
to the moonlit tree-tops,
that my blood may be cooled
by the wind.

Hallucination

I know this room,
and there are corridors:
the pictures, I have seen before;
the statues and those gems in cases
I have wandered by before,—
stood there silent and lonely
in a dream of years ago.

I know the dark of night is all around me;
my eyes are closed, and I am half asleep.
My wife breathes gently at my side.

But once again this old dream is within me,
and I am on the threshold waiting,
wondering, pleased, and fearful.
Where do those doors lead,
what rooms lie beyond them?
I venture. . . .

But my baby moves and tosses
from side to side,
and her need calls me to her.

Now I stand awake, unseeing,
in the dark,
and I move towards her cot. . . .
I shall not reach her . . . There is no direction. . . .
I shall walk on. . . .

"Immortal? . . . No"

Immortal? . . . No,
they cannot be, these people,
nor I.

Tired faces,
eyes that have never seen the world,
bodies that have never lived in air,
lips that have never minted speech,
they are the clipped and garbled,
blocking the highway.

They swarm and eddy
between the banks of glowing shops
towards the red meat,
the potherbs,
the cheapjacks,
or surge in
before the swift rush
of the clanging trams,—
pitiful, ugly, mean,
encumbering.

Immortal? . . .
In a wood,
watching the shadow of a bird
leap from frond to frond of bracken,
I am immortal.

But these?

"The grass is beneath my head"

The grass is beneath my head;
and I gaze
at the thronging stars
in the night.

They fall . . . they fall. . . .
I am overwhelmed,
and afraid.

Each leaf of the aspen
is caressed by the wind,
and each is crying.

And the perfume
of invisible roses
deepens the anguish.

Let a strong mesh of roots
feed the crimson of roses
upon my heart;
and then fold over the hollow
where all the pain was.

The Swan

Under the lily shadow
and the gold
and the blue and mauve
that the whin and the lilac
pour down on the water,
the fishes quiver.

Over the green cold leaves
and the rippled silver
and the tarnished copper
of its neck and beak,
toward the deep black water
beneath the arches,
the swan floats slowly.

Into the dark of the arch the swan floats
and into the black depth of my sorrow
it bears a white rose of flame.

Trees

Elm trees
and the leaf the boy in me hated
long ago—
rough and sandy.

Poplars
and their leaves,
tender, smooth to the fingers,
and a secret in their smell
I have forgotten.

Oaks
and forest glades,
heart aching with wonder, fear:
their bitter mast.

Willows
and the scented beetle
we put in our handkerchiefs;
and the roots of one

that spread into a river:
nakedness, water and joy.

Hawthorn,
white and odorous with blossom,
framing the quiet fields,
and swaying flowers and grasses,
and the hum of bees.

Oh, these are the things that are with me now,
in the town;
and I am grateful
for this minute of my manhood.

Accident

Dear one!
you sit there
in the corner of the carriage;
and you do not know me;
and your eyes forbid.

Is it the dirt, the squalor,
the wear of human bodies,
and the dead faces of our neighbours?
These are but symbols.

You are proud; I praise you;
your mouth is set; you see beyond us;
and you see nothing.

I have the vision of your calm, cold face,
and of the black hair that waves above it;
I watch you; I love you;
I desire you.

There is a quiet here
within the thud-thud of the wheels
upon the railway.

There is a quiet here
within my heart,
but tense and tender . . .

This is my station . . .

Fragment

. . . That night I loved you
in the candlelight.
Your golden hair
strewed the sweet whiteness of the pillows
and the counterpane.
O the darkness of the corners,
the warm air, and the stars
framed in the casement of the ships' lights!
The waves lapped into the harbour;
the boats creaked;
a man's voice sang out on the quay;
and you loved me.
In your love were the tall tree fuchsias,
the blue of the hortensias, the scarlet nasturtiums,
the trees on the hills,
the roads we had covered,
and the sea that had borne your body
before the rocks of Hartland.
You loved me with these
and with the kindness of people,
country folk, sailors and fishermen,
and the old lady who had lodged us and supped us.
You loved me with yourself
that was these and more,
changed as the earth is changed
into the bloom of flowers.

Houses

Evening and quiet:
a bird trills in the poplar trees
behind the house with the dark green door
across the road.

Into the sky,
the red earthenware and the galvanised iron chimneys
thrust their cowls.
The hoot of the steamers on the Thames is plain.

No wind;
the trees merge, green with green;
a car whirs by;
footsteps and voices take their pitch
in the key of dusk,
far-off and near, subdued.

Solid and square to the world
the houses stand,
their windows blocked with venetian blinds.

Nothing will move them.

Ogre

Through the open window can be seen
the poplars at the end of the garden
shaking in the wind,
a wall of green leaves so high
that the sky is shut off.

On the white table-cloth
a rose in a vase
—centre of a sphere of odour—
contemplates the crumbs and crusts
left from a meal:
cups, saucers, plates lie
here and there.

And a sparrow flies by the open window,
stops for a moment,
flutters his wings rapidly,
and climbs an aerial ladder
with his claws
that work close in
to his soft, brown-grey belly.

But behind the table is the face of a man.

The bird flies off.

Cones

The blue mist of after-rain
fills all the trees;

the sunlight gilds the tops
of the poplar spires, far off,
behind the houses.

Here a branch sways
and there
       a sparrow twitters.

The curtain's hem, rose-embroidered,
flutters, and half reveals
a burnt-red chimney pot.

The quiet in the room
bears patiently
a footfall on the street.

Gloom

I sat there in the dark
of the room and of my mind
thinking of men's treasons and bad faith,
sinking into the pit of my own weakness
before their strength of cunning.
Out over the gardens came the sound of some one
playing five-finger exercises on the piano.

Then
I gathered up within me all my powers
until outside of me was nothing:
I was all—
all stubborn, fighting sadness and revulsion.

And one came from the garden quietly,
and stood beside me.
She laid her hand on my hair;
she laid her cheek on my forehead,—
and caressed me with it;
but all my being rose to my forehead

to fight against this outside thing.
Something in me became angry;
withstood like a wall,
and would allow no entrance;
I hated her.

"What is the matter with you, dear?" she said.
"Nothing," I answered,
"I am thinking."
She stroked my hair and went away;
and I was still gloomy, angry, stubborn.

Then I thought:
she has gone away; she is hurt;
she does not know
what poison has been working in me.

Then I thought:
upstairs, her child is sleeping;
and I felt the presence
of the fields we had walked over, the roads we had followed,
the flowers we had watched together,
before it came.

She had touched my hair, and only then did I feel it;
And I loved her once again.

And I came away,
full of the sweet and bitter juices of life;
and I lit the lamp in my room,
and made this poem.

Terror

Eyes are tired;
the lamp burns,
and in its circle of light
papers and books lie
where chance and life
have placed them.

Silence sings all around me;
my head is bound with a band;
outside in the street a few footsteps;
a clock strikes the hour.

I gaze, and my eyes close,
slowly:

I doze; but the moment before sleep,
a voice calls my name
in my ear,
and the shock jolts my heart:
but when I open my eyes,
and look, first left, and then right . . .

no one is there.

Searchlight

There has been no sound of guns,
no roar of exploding bombs;
but the darkness has an edge
that grits the nerves of the sleeper.

He awakens;
nothing disturbs the stillness,
save perhaps the light, slow flap,
once only, of the curtain
dim in the darkness.

Yet there is something else
that drags him from his bed;
and he stands in the darkness
with his feet cold against the floor
and the cold air round his ankles.
He does not know why,
but he goes to the window and sees
a beam of light, miles high,
dividing the night into two before him,
still, stark and throbbing.

The houses and gardens beneath
lie under the snow
quiet and tinged with purple.

There has been no sound of guns,
no roar of exploding bombs;
only that watchfulness hidden among the snow-covered houses,
and that great beam thrusting back into heaven
the light taken from it.

Dusk

To J. C.

Here where the brown leaves fall
from elm and chestnut and plane-tree;
here where the brown leaves drift
along the paths to the lake
where the waterfowl breast the waves
that are ridged by the wind,—

you spoke of your art and life,
of men you had known who betrayed you,
men who fell short of friendship
and women who fell short of love;
but, abiding beyond them, your art
held you to life, transformed it, became it,
and so you were free.

And I told you of all my weakness,—
my growing strength to resist
the appeal to my heart and eyes
of sorrowful, beautiful things;
and the strength of this outer husk
I had permitted to grow and protect me
was its pitiful measure.

You said: There are cracks in the husk.
It grew to your measure perhaps once;
but you are now breaking through it, and soon
it will fall apart and away from you.
Like a tree content with its fate,
you would not have known it was there
if it had grown to remain.

The cold wind blew the brown leaves
on to the lovers beneath,
who crept closer together for warmth
and closer still for love.

The peacocks perched in the branches
hawked their harsh cry at the golden
round moon that loomed over the tree-tops.

And the sound of our feet on the gravel
for a time was answer enough
to the broken mesh of our thoughts.

I said: I have wife and children,
a girl and a boy: I love them;
the gold of their hair is all the gold
of my thoughts; the blue of their eyes
is all the purity of my vision;
the rhythm of their life is more to be watched
than the cadences of my poems.

And you asked me:
Have you taken refuge behind them?
Do you not fear to lose your life
in saving it for them?
Be brave! Be brave! The waters are deep,
the waves run high; but you are a swimmer:
strike out!

The cold wind blew the brown leaves
deeper and deeper into the dusk;
the peacocks had hushed their cries;
the moon had turned her gold into silver,
and between the black lace of two trees
one star shone clearly.

O night!
have I deserved your beauty?

Evil

   The mist of the evening is rose
In the dying sun,
And the street is quiet between its rows of plane-trees,
And the walls of the gardens
With the laurel bushes.

   I walk along in a dream,
Half aware
Of the empty black of the windows.

   One window I pass by.
It is not empty:
Something shows from it—white, I feel, and round—
Something that pulls me back
To gaze, still dreaming,
To gaze and to wake and stare
At a naked woman—
Oh, beautiful!
Alone in the window.

   Is there a sign?
Does she call me?
What is the lure?

   She does not move.

   And I crawl to the gate, and stop,
And open the gate, again stopping,
And crawl again up the stone steps—
Fear driving my heart mad—
Up to the door.

Door, do not open—
Though I beat you with my fists!

FORD MADOX HUEFFER
(1873–1939)

In the Little Old Market-Place

(To the Memory of A. V.)

It rains, it rains,
From gutters and drains
And gargoyles and gables:
It drips from the tables
That tell us the tolls upon grains,
Oxen, asses, sheep, turkeys and fowls
Set into the rain-soaked wall
Of the old Town Hall.

The mountains being so tall
And forcing the town on the river,
The market's so small
That, with the wet cobbles, dark arches and all,
The owls
(For in dark rainy weather the owls fly out
Well before four), so the owls
In the gloom
Have too little room
And brush by the saint on the fountain
In veering about.

The poor saint on the fountain!
Supported by plaques of the giver
To whom we're beholden;
His name was de Sales
And his wife's name von Mangel.

(Now is he a saint or archangel?)
He stands on a dragon
On a ball, on a column
Gazing up at the vines on the mountain:
And his falchion is golden
And his wings are all golden.
He bears golden scales
And in spite of the coils of his dragon, without hint of alarm or invective
Looks up at the mists on the mountain.

(Now what saint or archangel
Stands winged on a dragon,
Bearing golden scales and a broad bladed sword all golden?
Alas, my knowledge
Of all the saints of the college,
Of all these glimmering, olden
Sacred and misty stories
Of angels and saints and old glories . . .
Is sadly defective.)
The poor saint on the fountain . . .

On top of his column
Gazes up sad and solemn.
But is it towards the top of the mountain
Where the spindrifty haze is
That he gazes?
Or is it into the casement
Where the girl sits sewing?
There's no knowing.

Hear it rain!
And from eight leaden pipes in the ball he stands on
That has eight leaden and copper bands on,
There gurgle and drain
Eight driblets of water down into the basin.

And he stands on his dragon
And the girl sits sewing
High, very high in her casement
And before her are many geraniums in a parket
All growing and blowing
In box upon box
From the gables right down to the basement
With frescoes and carvings and paint . . .

The poor saint!
It rains and it rains,
In the market there isn't an ox,
And in all the emplacement
For waggons there isn't a waggon,
Not a stall for a grape or a raisin,
Not a soul in the market
Save the saint on his dragon
With the rain dribbling down in the basin,
And the maiden that sews in the casement.

They are still and alone,
Mutterseelens alone,
And the rain dribbles down from his heels and his crown,
From wet stone to wet stone.
It's grey as at dawn,
And the owls, grey and fawn,
Call from the little town hall
With its arch in the wall,
Where the fire-hooks are stored.

From behind the flowers of her casement
That's all gay with the carvings and paint,
The maiden gives a great yawn,
But the poor saint—
No doubt he's as bored!
Stands still on his column
Uplifting his sword
With never the ease of a yawn
From wet dawn to wet dawn . . .

The Starling

It's an odd thing how one changes . . .
Walking along the upper ranges
Of this land of plains,
In this month of rains,
On a drying road where the poplars march along,
Suddenly,
With a rush of wings flew down a company,
A multitude, throng upon throng,
Of starlings,

Successive orchestras of song,
Flung, like the babble of surf,
On to the roadside turf—

And so, for a mile, for a mile and a half—a long way,
Flight follows flight
Thro' the still grey light
Of the steel-grey day,
Whirling beside the road in clamorous crowds,
Never near, never far, in the shade of the poplars and clouds.

It's an odd thing how one changes . . .
And what strikes me now as most strange is:
After the starlings had flown
Over the plain and were gone,
There was one of them stayed on alone
In the trees; it chattered on high,
Lifting its bill to the sky,
Distending its throat,
Crooning harsh note after note,
In soliloquy,
Sitting alone.

And after a hush
It gurgled as gurgled a well,
Warbled as warbles a thrush,
Had a try at the sound of a bell
And mimicked a jay. . . .
But I,
Whilst the starling mimicked on high
Pulsing its throat and its wings,
I went on my way
Thinking of things,
Onwards and over the range
And that's what is strange.

I went down 'twixt tobacco and grain,
Descending the chequer board plain
Where the apples and maize are;
Under the loopholed gate
In the village wall
Where the goats clatter over the cobbles
And the intricate, straw-littered ways are . . .
The ancient watchman hobbles
Cloaked, with his glasses of horn at the end of his nose,

Wearing velvet short hose
And a three-cornered hat on his pate,
And his pike-staff and all.
And he carries a proclamation,
An invitation,
To great and small,
Man and beast
To a wedding feast,
And he carries a bell and rings . . .
From the steeple looks down a saint,
From a doorway a queenly peasant
Looks out, in her bride-gown of lace
And her sister, a quaint little darling
Who twitters and chirps like a starling.

And this little old place,
It's so quaint,
It's so pleasant;
And the watch bell rings, and the church bell rings
And the wedding procession draws nigh,
Bullock carts, fiddlers and goods.
But I
Pass on my way to the woods
Thinking of things.

Years ago I'd have stayed by the starling,
Marking the iridescence of his throat,
Marvelling at the change of his note;
I'd have said to the peasant child: "Darling
Here's a groschen and give me a kiss" . . . I'd have stayed
To sit with the bridesmaids at table,
And have taken my chance
Of a dance
With the bride in her laces
Or the maids with the blonde, placid faces
And ribbons and crants in the stable . . .

But the church bell still rings
And I'm far away out on the plain,
In the grey weather amongst the tobacco and grain,
And village and gate and wall
Are a long grey line with the church over all
And miles and miles away in the sky
The starlings go wheeling round on high

Over the distant ranges.
The violin strings
Thrill away and the day grows more grey.
And I . . . I stand thinking of things.
Yes, it's strange how one changes.

Antwerp

I

Gloom!
An October like November;
August a hundred thousand hours,
And all September,
A hundred thousand, dragging sunlit days,
And half October like a thousand years . . .
And doom!
That then was Antwerp . . .
                    In the name of God,
How could they do it?
Those souls that usually dived
Into the dirty caverns of mines;
Who usually hived
In whitened hovels; under ragged poplars;
Who dragged muddy shovels, over the grassy mud,
Lumbering to work over the greasy sods . . .
Those men there, with the appearance of clods
Were the bravest men that a usually listless priest of God
Ever shrived . . .
And it is not for us to make them an anthem.
If we found words there would come no wind that would fan them
To a tune that the trumpets might blow it,
Shrill through the heaven that's ours or yet Allah's,
Or the wide halls of any Valhallas.
We can make no such anthem. So that all that is ours
For inditing in sonnets, pantoums, elegiacs, or lays
Is this:
"In the name of God, how could they do it?"

II

For there is no new thing under the sun,
Only this uncomely man with a smoking gun

In the gloom. . . .
What the devil will he gain by it?
Digging a hole in the mud and standing all day in the rain by it
Waiting his doom;
The sharp blow, the swift outpouring of the blood
Till the trench of gray mud
Is turned to a brown purple drain by it.
Well, there have been scars
Won in many wars,
Punic,
Lacedæmonian, wars of Napoleon, wars for faith, wars for honor, for
    love, for possession,
But this Belgian man in his ugly tunic,
His ugly round cap, shooting on, in a sort of obsession,
Overspreading his miserable land,
Standing with his wet gun in his hand. . . .
Doom!
He finds that in a sudden scrimmage,
And lies, an unsightly lump on the sodden grass . . .
An image that shall take long to pass!

III

For the white-limbed heroes of Hellas ride by upon their horses
Forever through our brains.
The heroes of Cressy ride by upon their stallions;
And battalions and battalions and battalions—
The Old Guard, the Young Guard, the men of Minden and of
    Waterloo,
Pass, for ever staunch,
Stand, for ever true;
And the small man with the large paunch,
And the gray coat, and the large hat, and the hands behind the back,
Watches them pass
In our minds for ever. . . .
But that clutter of sodden corses
On the sodden Belgian grass—
That is a strange new beauty.

IV

With no especial legends of marchings or triumphs or duty,
Assuredly that is the way of it,
The way of beauty. . . .
And that is the highest word you can find to say of it.

For you cannot praise it with words
Compounded of lyres and swords,
But the thought of the gloom and the rain
And the ugly coated figure, standing beside a drain,
Shall eat itself into your brain:
And you will say of all heroes, "They fought like the Belgians!"
And you will say, "He wrought like a Belgian his fate out of gloom."
And you will say, "He bought like a Belgian
His doom."
And that shall be an honorable name;
"Belgian" shall be an honorable word;
As honorable as the fame of the sword,
As honorable as the mention of the many-chorded lyre,
And his old coat shall seem as beautiful as the fabrics woven in Tyre.

V

And what in the world did they bear it for?
I don't know.
And what in the world did they dare it for?
Perhaps that is not for the likes of me to understand.
They could very well have watched a hundred legions go
Over their fields and between their cities
Down into more southerly regions.
They could very well have let the legions pass through their woods,
And have kept their lives and their wives and their children and cattle
    and goods.
I don't understand.
Was it just love of their land?
Oh, poor dears!
Can any man so love his land?
Give them a thousand thousand pities
And rivers and rivers of tears
To wash off the blood from the cities of Flanders.

VI

This is Charing Cross;
It is midnight;
There is a great crowd
And no light—
A great crowd, all black, that hardly whispers aloud.
Surely, that is a dead woman—a dead mother!
She has a dead face;
She is dressed all in black;

She wanders to the book-stall and back,
At the back of the crowd;
And back again and again back,
She sways and wanders.

This is Charing Cross;
It is one o'clock.
There is still a great cloud, and very little light;
Immense shafts of shadows over the black crowd
That hardly whispers aloud. . . .
And now! . . . That is another dead mother,
And there is another and another and another. . . .
And little children, all in black,
All with dead faces, waiting in all the waiting-places,
Wandering from the doors of the waiting-room
In the dim gloom.
These are the women of Flanders:
They await the lost.
They await the lost that shall never leave the dock;
They await the lost that shall never again come by the train
To the embraces of all these women with dead faces;
They await the lost who lie dead in trench and barrier and fosse,
In the dark of the night.
This is Charing Cross; it is past one of the clock;
There is very little light.

There is so much pain.

 L'Envoi:
And it was for this that they endured this gloom;
This October like November,
That August like a hundred thousand hours,
And that September,
A hundred thousand dragging sunlit days
And half October like a thousand years. . . .
Oh, poor dears!

T. E. HULME
(1883–1917)

Autumn

A touch of cold in the Autumn night—
I walked abroad,
And saw the ruddy moon lean over a hedge
Like a red-faced farmer.
I did not stop to speak, but nodded,
And round about were the wistful stars
With white faces like town children.

Above the Dock

Above the quiet dock in mid night,
Tangled in the tall mast's corded height,
Hangs the moon. What seemed so far away
Is but a child's balloon, forgotten after play.

The Embankment

(The fantasia of a fallen gentleman on a cold, bitter night.)

Once, in finesse of fiddles found I ecstasy,
In the flash of gold heels on the hard pavement.
Now see I
That warmth's the very stuff of poesy.

Oh, God, make small
The old star-eaten blanket of the sky,
That I may fold it round me and in comfort lie.

Conversion

Lighthearted I walked into the valley wood
In the time of hyacinths,
Till beauty like a scented cloth
Cast over, stifled me. I was bound
Motionless and faint of breath
By loveliness that is her own eunuch.

Now pass I to the final river
Ignominiously, in a sack, without sound,
As any peeping Turk to the Bosphorus.

JAMES JOYCE
(1882–1941)

I Hear an Army

I hear an army charging upon the land,
And the thunder of horses plunging; foam about their knees:
Arrogant, in black armour, behind them stand,
Disdaining the rains, with fluttering whips, the Charioteers.

They cry into the night their battle name:
I moan in sleep when I hear afar their whirling laughter.
They cleave the gloom of dreams, a blinding flame,
Clanging, clanging upon the heart as upon an anvil.

They come shaking in triumph their long grey hair:
They come out of the sea and run shouting by the shore.
My heart, have you no wisdom thus to despair?
My love, my love, my love, why have you left me alone?

"Silently she's combing"

Silently she's combing,
   Combing her long hair,
Silently and graciously,
   With many a pretty air.

The sun is in the willow leaves
   And on the dappled grass,
And still she's combing her long hair
   Before the looking-glass.

I pray you, cease to comb out,
    Comb out your long hair,
For I have heard of witchery
    Under a pretty air,

That makes as one thing to the lover
    Staying and going hence,
All fair, with many a pretty air
    And many a negligence.

"O, it was out by Donnycarney"

O, it was out by Donnycarney
    When the bat flew from tree to tree
My love and I did walk together;
    And sweet were the words she said to me.

Along with us the summer wind
    Went murmuring—O, happily!—
But softer than the breath of summer
    Was the kiss she gave to me.

ALFRED KREYMBORG
(1883–1966)

Cézanne

Our door was shut to the noon-day heat.
We could not see him.
We might not have heard him either—
Resting, dozing, dreaming pleasantly.
But his step was tremendous—
Are mountains on the march?

He was no man who passed;
But a great faithful horse
Dragging a load
Up the hill.

Clavichord

If you stand where I stand—
in my boudoir—
(don't mind my shaving—
I can't afford a barber)—
you can see into her boudoir—
you can see milady—
her back, her green smock, the bench she loves—
her hair always down in the morning—
black, and nearly as long as the curtains—
with ringlets at the tips—

the hairdresser called this A.M.—
him I have to, I want to afford.
Unhappily, you can't see her face—
only the back of her small round head—
and a glint of her ears, two glints—
but her hands, alas, not her hands, though
happily, you can hear them.
It isn't a clavichord—
only a satinwood square—
bought cheap at an auction—
but it might be, you'd think it,
a clavichord, bequeathed by the past—
it sounds quite like feathers.
Bach? Yes, who else could that be—
whom else would you have in the morning—
with the sun and milady?
Grave? Yes, but so is the sun—
not always? No, but please don't ponder—
listen, hear the theme—
hear it dig into the earth of harmonies.
A dissonance? No, it's only a stone—
which powders into particles with the rest.
Now follow the theme—
down, down, into the soil—
calling, evoking the spirit of birth—
you hear those new tones—
that sprinkle, that burst—
roulade and arpeggio?
Gently now, firmly—
with solemn persuasion—
hiding a whimsic raillery—
(does a dead king raise his forefinger?)—
though they would, though they might—
no phrase can escape—
the theme rules.
Unhappy? No,
they ought to be happy—
each is because of, in spite of, the other—
that is democracy—
he can't spare a particle—
that priest of the morning sun.
A mistake? Yes indeed, but—
all the more human—

would you have her drum like a schoolmaster—
abominable right note at the right time—
in the morning, so early—
or ever at all?—
she'll play it again—
oh don't, please don't clap—
you'll disturb them!
Here, try my tobacco—
good, a deep pipeful, eh?—
an aromatic blend—
my other extravagance—
yes, I'll join you, but wait—
I must first dry my face!

Tiger-Lily

To have reached
the ultimate top
of the stalk,
single, tall, fragile;
to hang like a bell,
through sheer weight
of oneself,
rather than pride of
it being the top,
no higher to go,
rather than modesty
of it being
only a stalk,
one among myriads;
to have one's six petals,
refusing the straight
for the curve,
dipping mere pin-pricks
around the horizon;
to have six tongues,
which, however the mood
of the wind may blow,
refuse to clap into sound;
and to keep, withal,
one's finest marvel,

one's passionate specks,
invisible:
tiger-lily,
if I bow,
it is not
in imitation;
it is
in recognition
of true being.

Clay

I wish
there were thirteen
gods in the sky,
even twelve might achieve it:

Or even
one god
in me:

Alone,
I can't shape
an image of her.

Image

Showing her immortal—
it's mine to do—
but I can't.
Shaping her—
just as she is—
a thing
to turn a glance
to an eternity—
mood shaping form—
imperishable—
it's there—
I can see it—
but I can't say it.

There's no secret about it—
she tells it
every breathing, breathless moment—
I can hear it—
but I can't say it.

What can my mere
body and scrivening
leave you, if
it doesn't leave you her?

If I could transcribe
one infinitesimal phase
of the trillion-starred endowment
which comes tumbling
out of simply trying to look at her,
or out of catching a glance,
slyly pointed,
trying to look at me,
stirring a trillion-starred emotion,
vibrating like a bell
across endless tides of endless seas—
I'd do it—
but I can't.

I love her so much,
I can't do anything else.

Screen Dance: For Rihani

Its posterior pushing
its long thin body,
a procession of waves lifting its head—
a green caterpillar:

Its roots digging and drinking,
the sap driving outward and up,
shaking its yellow head—
the mountain top of a tree:

Idling along in the blue,
an easy white holiday,
swimming away towards the rim of the bowl—
a cloud:
Dipping and twirling,
soaring, floating, following after—
a butterfly.

D. H. LAWRENCE
(1885–1930)

Cherry Robbers

Under the long, dark boughs, like jewels red
   In the hair of an Eastern girl
Shine strings of crimson cherries, as if had bled
   Blood-drops beneath each curl.

Under the glistening cherries, with folded wings
   Three dead birds lie:
Pale-breasted throstles and a blackbird, robberlings
   Stained with red dye.

Under the haystack a girl stands laughing at me,
   With cherries hung round her ears—
Offering me her scarlet fruit: I will see
   If she has any tears.

Honeymoon

I wonder, can the night go by,
Can this shot arrow of travel fly
Shaft-golden with light, at the joint of the sky
   And out into morning,
Without delivering once my eye

From sight of me, without once your turning
   Your face toward my agony?

What is it then that you can see,
As at the window endlessly
You watch the fire sparks swirl and flee
   And the night look through?
The sight of you peering lonely there
Oppresses me, I can scarcely bear
   To share the train with you.

Still I must sit in agony
As you crouch and turn away from me,
In torture of your proximity—
   Oh, I would not love you—
How I have longed for this night in the train,
Yet every fibre of me cries in pain
   Now to God to remove you.

But surely, surely I know that still
Come on us another night, you will
Lift up your measure to me to fill—
   Touch cups and drink.
It is only I find it hard to bear,
To have you sitting averted there
   With all your senses ashrink.

But my dear love, when another night
Comes on us, you'll lift your fingers white
And strip me naked, touch be alight,
   Light, light all over?
For I ache most earnestly for your touch,
I am ashamed that I ache so much
   For you, my lover.

For night after night with a blemish of day
Unblown and unblossomed has withered away:
Come another night, come to-morrow, say
   Will you pluck it apart?
Will you loose the heavy, weary bud
To the fire and rain, will you take the flood
   Of me to heart,
   To the very heart?

Illicit

In front of the sombre mountains, a faint, lost ribbon of rainbow,
And between us and it, the thunder;
And down below, in the green wheat, the labourers
Stand like dark stumps, still in the green wheat.

You are near to me, and your naked feet in their sandals,
And through the scent of the balcony's naked timber
I distinguish the scent of your hair; so now the limber
Lightning falls from heaven.

Adown the pale-green, glacier-river floats
A dark boat through the gloom—and whither?
The thunder roars. But still we have each other.
The naked lightnings in the heaven dither
And disappear. What have we but each other?
The boat has gone.

Fireflies in the Corn

A Woman taunts her Lover

Look at the little darlings in the corn!
The rye is taller than you, who think yourself
So high and mighty: look how its heads are borne
Dark and proud in the sky, like a number of knights
Passing with spears and pennants and manly scorn.

And always likely!—Oh, if I could ride
With my head held high-serene against the sky
Do you think I'd have a creature like you at my side
With your gloom and your doubt that you love me? O darling rye,
How I adore you for your simple pride!

And those bright fireflies wafting in between
And over the swaying cornstalks, just above
All their dark-feathered helmets, like little green
Stars come low and wandering here for love
Of this dark earth, and wandering all serene—!

How I adore you, you happy things, you dears
Riding the air and carrying all the time
Your little lanterns behind you: it cheers
My heart to see you settling and trying to climb
The cornstalks, tipping with fire their spears.

All over the corn's dim motion, against the blue
Dark sky of night, the wandering glitter, the swarm
Of questing brilliant things:—you joy, you true
Spirit of careless joy: ah, how I warm
My poor and perished soul at the joy of you!

The Man answers and she mocks

You 're a fool, woman. I love you and you know I do!
    —Lord, take his love away, it makes him whine.
And I give you everything that you want me to.
    —Lord, dear Lord, do you think he ever *can* shine?

A Woman and Her Dead Husband

Ah, stern cold man,
How can you lie so relentless hard
While I wash you with weeping water!
Ah, face, carved hard and cold,
You have been like this, on your guard
Against me, since death began.

You masquerader!
How can you shame to act this part
Of unswerving indifference to me?
It is not you; why disguise yourself
Against me, to break my heart,
You evader?

You've a warm mouth,
A good warm mouth always sooner to soften
Even than your sudden eyes.
Ah cruel, to keep your mouth
Relentless, however often
I kiss it in drouth.

You are not he.
Who are you, lying in his place on the bed
And rigid and indifferent to me?
His mouth, though he laughed or sulked
Was always warm and red
And good to me.

And his eyes could see
The white moon hang like a breast revealed
By the slipping shawl of stars,
Could see the small stars tremble
As the heart beneath did wield
Systole, diastole.

And he showed it me
So, when he made his love to me;
And his brows like rocks on the sea jut out,
And his eyes were deep like the sea
With shadow, and he looked at me,
Till I sank in him like the sea,
Awfully.

Oh, he was multiform—
Which then was he among the manifold?
The gay, the sorrowful, the seer?
I have loved a rich race of men in one—
—But not this, this never-warm
Metal-cold—!

Ah, masquerader!
With your steel face white-enamelled
Were you he, after all, and I never
Saw you or felt you in kissing?
—Yet sometimes my heart was trammelled
With fear, evader!

You will not stir,
Nor hear me, not a sound.
—Then it was you—
And all this time you were
Like this when I lived with you.
    It is not true,
    I am frightened, I am frightened of you
    And of everything.
    O God!—God too
    Has deceived me in everything,
    In everything.

The Mowers

There's four men mowing down by the river;
　　I can hear the sound of the scythe strokes, four
Sharp breaths swishing:—yea, but I
　　Am sorry for what's i' store.

The first man out o' the four that's mowin'
　　Is mine: I mun claim him once for all:
—But I'm sorry for him, on his young feet, knowin'
　　None o' the trouble he's led to stall.

As he sees me bringin' the dinner, he lifts
　　His head as proud as a deer that looks
Shoulder-deep out o' th' corn: and wipes
　　His scythe blade bright, unhooks

His scythe stone, an' over the grass to me!
　　—Lad, tha's gotten a chilt in me,
An' a man an' a father tha 'lt ha'e to be,
　　My young slim lad, an' I'm sorry for thee.

Scent of Irises

A faint, sickening scent of irises
Persists all morning. Here in a jar on the table
A fine proud spike of purple irises
Rising above the class-room litter, makes me unable
To see the class's lifted and bended faces
Save in a broken pattern, amid purple and gold and sable.

I can smell the gorgeous bog-end, in its breathless
Dazzle of may-blobs, when the marigold glare overcast
You with fire on your brow and your cheeks and your chin as you
　　dipped
Your face in your marigold bunch, to touch and contrast
Your own dark mouth with the bridal faint lady-smocks
Dissolved in the golden sorcery you should not outlast.

You amid the bog-end's yellow incantation,
You sitting in the cowslips of the meadows above,
—Me, your shadow on the bog-flame, flowery may-blobs,
Me full length in the cowslips, muttering you love—

You, your soul like a lady-smock, lost, evanescent,
You, with your face all rich, like the sheen on a dove—!

You are always asking, do I remember, remember
The buttercup bog-end where the flowers rose up
And kindled you over deep with a coat of gold?
You ask again, do the healing days close up
The open darkness which then drew us in,
The dark that swallows all, and nought throws up.

You upon the dry, dead beech-leaves, in the fire of night
Burnt like a sacrifice;—you invisible—
Only the fire of darkness, and the scent of you!
—And yes, thank God, it still is possible
The healing days shall close the darkness up
Wherein I breathed you like a smoke or dew.

Like vapour, dew, or poison. Now, thank God,
The golden fire has gone, and your face is ash
Indistinguishable in the grey, chill day,
The night has burnt you out, at last the good
Dark fire burns on untroubled without clash
Of you upon the dead leaves saying me yea.

Green

The sky was apple-green,
The sky was green wine held up in the sun,
The moon was a golden petal between.

She opened her eyes, and green
They shone, clear like flowers undone,
For the first time, now for the first time seen.

Erinnyes

There has been so much noise,
Bleeding and shouting and dying,
Clamour of death.

There are so many dead,
Many have died unconsenting,
Their ghosts are angry, unappeased.

So many ghosts among us,
Invisible, yet strong,
Between me and thee, so many ghosts of the slain.

They come back, over the white sea, in the mist,
Invisible, trooping home, the unassuaged ghosts
Endlessly returning on the uneasy sea.

They set foot on this land to which they have the right,
They return relentlessly, in the silence one knows their tread,
Multitudinous, endless, the ghosts coming home again.

They watch us, they press on us,
They press their claim upon us,
They are angry with us.

What do they want?
We are driven mad,
Madly we rush hither and thither:
Shouting, "Revenge, Revenge,"
Crying, "Pour out the blood of the foe,"
Seeking to appease with blood the insistent ghosts.

Out of blood rise up new ghosts,
Grey, stern, angry, unsatisfied,
The more we slay and are slain, the more we raise up new ghosts
    against us.

Till we are mad with terror, seeing the slain
Victorious, grey, grisly ghosts in our streets,
Grey, unappeased ghosts seated in the music-halls.
The dead triumphant, and the quick cast down,
The dead, unassuaged and angry, silencing us,
Making us pale and bloodless, without resistance.

What do they want, the ghosts, what is it
They demand as they stand in menace over against us?
How shall we now appease whom we have raised up?

Since from blood poured out rise only ghosts again,
What shall we do, what shall we give to them?
What do they want, forever there on our threshold?

Must we open the doors, and admit them, receive them home,
And in the silence, reverently, welcome them,
And give them place and honour and service meet?

For one year's space, attend on our angry dead,
Soothe them with service and honour, and silence meet,
Strengthen, prepare them for the journey hence,
Then lead them to the gates of the unknown,
And bid farewell, oh stately travellers,
And wait till they are lost upon our sight.

Then we shall turn us home again to life
Knowing our dead are fitly housed in death,
Not roaming here disconsolate, angrily.

And we shall have new peace in this our life,
New joy to give more life, new bliss to live,
Sure of our dead in the proud halls of death.

In Trouble and Shame

I look at the sweeling sunset
And wish I could go also
Through the red doors beyond the black-purple bar.

I wish that I could go
Through the red doors where I could put off
My shame like shoes in the porch
My pain like garments,
And leave my flesh discarded lying
Like luggage of some departed traveller
Gone one knows not where.

Then I would turn round
And seeing my cast-off body lying like lumber,
I would laugh with joy.

Brooding Grief

A yellow leaf from the darkness
Hops like a frog before me—
—Why should I start and stand still?

I was watching the woman that bore me
Stretched in the brindled darkness
Of the sick-room, rigid with will
To die—
And the quick leaf tore me
Back to this rainy swill
Of leaves and lamps and traffic mingled before me.

Restlessness

At the open door of the room I stand and look at the night,
Hold my hand to catch the raindrops, that slant into sight,
Arriving grey from the darkness above suddenly into the light of the
    room.
I will escape from the hollow room, the box of light,
And be out in the bewildering darkness, which is always fecund,
    which might
Mate my hungry soul with a germ of its womb.

I will go out to the night, as a man goes down to the shore
To draw his net through the surf's thin line, at the dawn before
The sun warms the sea, little, lonely and sad, sifting the sobbing tide.
I will sift the surf that edges the night, with my net, the four
Strands of my eyes and my lips and my hands and my feet, sifting the
    store
Of flotsam until my soul is tired or satisfied.

I will catch in my eyes' quick net
The faces of all the women as they go past,
Bend over them with my soul, to cherish the wet
Cheeks and wet hair a moment, saying: "Is it you?"
Looking earnestly under the dark umbrellas, held fast
Against the wind; and if, where the lamplight blew
Its rainy swill about us, she answered me
With a laugh and a merry wildness that it was she
Who was seeking me, and had found me at last to free

Me now from the stunting bonds of my chastity,
How glad I should be!

Moving along in the mysterious ebb of the night
Pass the men whose eyes are shut like anemones in a dark pool;
Why don't they open with vision and speak to me, what have they in
    sight?
Why do I wander aimless among them, desirous fool?

I can always linger over the huddled books on the stalls,
Always gladden my amorous fingers with the touch of their leaves,
Always kneel in courtship to the shelves in the doorways, where falls
The shadow, always offer myself to one mistress, who always receives.

But oh, it is not enough, it is all no good.
There is something I want to feel in my running blood,
Something I want to touch; I must hold my face to the rain,
I must hold my face to the wind, and let it explain
Me its life as it hurries in secret.
I will trail my hands again through the drenched, cold leaves
Till my hands are full of the chillness and touch of leaves,
Till at length they induce me to sleep, and to forget.

Terra Nuova

I

And so I cross into another world,
shyly and in homage linger for an invitation
from this unknown that I would trespass on.

I am very glad, and all alone in the world,
all alone, and very glad, in a new world
where I am disembarked at last.

I could cry for joy, because I am in a new world, just ventured in;
I could cry with joy, and quite freely, there is nobody to know.

And whosoever the unknown people of this unknown world will be,
they will never understand my weeping for joy to be adventuring
    among them,
because it will be a gesture of the old world I am making,
which they will not understand, because it is quite, quite foreign to
    them.

II

I was so weary of the world
I was so sick of it.
Everything was tainted with myself;
sky, trees, flowers, birds, water,
people, houses, streets, vehicles, machines,
nations, armies, war, peace-making,
work, recreation, governing, anarchy,
it was all tainted with myself, I knew it all to start with
because it was all myself.

When I gathered flowers, I knew it was myself gathering my own
    flowers;
when I went in a train, I knew myself going in my own train;
when I heard the cannon of the war, my ears listened to my own
    cannon,
when I saw the torn dead, I knew it was my own torn dead body,
it was all me, I had done it all.

III

I shall never forget the maniacal horror of it, in the end,
when everything was me, I knew it all already, anticipated it all;
because I was the author and the result
I was the God and the creation at once;
Creator, I looked at my creation,
Created, I looked at myself, the Creator.
It was a maniacal horror in the end.

IV

I was the lover, I kissed the woman,
and, God of horror, I was kissing also myself;
I was a father and begetter of children,
and oh, oh horror, I was begetting myself in my own body.

V

At last came death, sufficiency of death,
and that at last relieved me, I died.
I buried my beloved—it was good; I buried myself and was dead.
War came, and hatred, and every hand raised to murder.
Good, very good, every hand raised to murder!
Very good, very good, I am also a murderer! It is my desire.

It is good; I can strike and strike and see them all fall,
the mutilated, horror-struck youths, in a multitude,

one and another, and then in clusters together,
smashed, and broken with blood, and then burned in heaps,
going up in fetid smoke to get rid of them,
the murdered bodies of youths and men and me, in heaps,
heaps, in heaps, in horrible reeking heaps,
till it is almost enough, till I am killed perhaps:

thousands and thousands of gaping, hideous foul dead,
that are youths and men and me, being burned with oil, and
      consumed
in corrupt thick smoke, that rolls
and taints and blackens the sky, till at last
it is dark, as dark as night, or death, or hell,
and I am dead, and trodden like earth in the sodden earth,
dead, and trodden to nought in the sour black earth,
dead, and trodden to nought, trodden to nought.

VI

Ah, but it is good to have died and been trodden out!
Trodden to nought in black, dead earth,
quite to nought
to nothing;
absolutely to nothing.

VII

When it is quite, quite nothing, then it is everything.
When I am trodden quite out, quite, quite out,
every vestige gone—then I am here,
discovered, setting my foot on another world,
landed, claiming another terrestrial life,
disembarked from the voyage of death—not risen, not born again,
but disembarked from out the horrible foul ship, into a new heaven
      and earth,
new beyond knowledge of newness, alive beyond life,
glad beyond glory and furthest conception of pride,
living where life was never yet dreamed, where nothing was hinted at,
that is, now, in the world, with me and with life.

VIII

I put out my hand in the night, one night, and my hand
touched that which was verily not me,
verily it was not me.
Where I had been, was a sudden blaze,

a sudden flaring blaze of new being.
So I put my hand out further, again, and further
felt that which was not I,
it verily was not I.
It was the Unknown.

I was a blaze leaping up,
I was a burst of light, a tiger,
I was greedy, I was mad for the Unknown,
I, new-landed, new-risen, starved, disembarked from the tomb,
starved from a life of selfless consuming myself,
here was I now, arriving, with my hand stretched out
and touching the real Unknown, the Unknown, the Unknown.

And oh, I can only say
that I can touch, I can feel the Unknown;
I, the first comer.
Cortes, Pisarro, Columbus, they are nothing,
I am the first Comer
I am the discoverer
I have found the other world.

Eureka!
The Unknown, the Unknown!
I am thrown upon the shore,
I am covering myself with the sand,
I am filling my mouth with the earth,
I am burrowing my body into the soil:
the Unknown!

IX

It was the flank of my wife
I touched with my hand, I clutched with my hand,
rising, reaching from the tomb,
it was the flank of my wife, whom I had married years ago,
at whose side I have lain for a thousand nights,
and all the while, she was I, she was I,
I touched her, it was I who touched and I who was touched.

Yet rising from the tomb, flung from the ship,
stretching out my hand, my hand flung like a drowning man's hand
      on the shore,
I touched her flank, and knew myself carried by the current in death
over to the new world, touching the other shore,

flotsam, jetsam, thrown and washed back on the shore,
yet grasping the new world,
clutching to climb out on the new and timeless world.

Service of All the Dead

Between the avenue of cypresses
All in their scarlet capes and surplices
Of linen, go the chaunting choristers,
The priests in gold and black, the villagers.

And all along the path to the cemetery
The round dark heads of men crowd silently;
And black-scarfed faces of women-folk wistfully
Watch at the banner of death, and the mystery.

And at the foot of a grave a father stands
With sunken head and forgotten, folded hands;
And at the foot of a grave a mother kneels
With pale shut face, nor neither hears nor feels

The coming of the chaunting choristers
Between the avenue of cypresses,
The silence of the many villagers,
The candle-flames beside the surplices.

Gloire de Dijon

When she rises in the morning
I linger to watch her;
She spreads the bath-cloth underneath the window
And the sunbeams catch her
Glistening white on the shoulders,
While down her sides the mellow
Golden shadow glows as
She stoops to the sponge, and her swung breasts
Sway like full-blown yellow
Gloire de Dijon roses.

She drips herself with water, and her shoulders
Glisten as silver, they crumple up
Like wet and falling roses, and I listen
For the sluicing of their rain-dishevelled petals.
In the window full of sunlight
Concentrates her golden shadow
Fold on fold, until it glows as
Mellow as the glory roses.

Nostalgia

The waning moon looks upward, this grey night
Sheers round the heavens in one smooth curve
Of easy sailing. Odd red wicks serve
To show where the ships at sea move out of sight.

This place is palpable me, for here I was born
Of this self-same darkness. Yet the shadowy house below
Is out of bounds, and only the old ghosts know
I have come—they whimper about me, welcome and mourn.

My father suddenly died in the harvesting corn,
And the place is no longer ours. Watching, I hear
No sound from the strangers; the place is dark, and fear
Opens my eyes till the roots of my vision seem torn.

Can I go nearer, never towards the door?
The ghosts and I, we mourn together, and shrink
In the shadow of the cart-shed—hovering on the brink
For ever, to enter the homestead no more.

Is it irrevocable? Can I really not go
Through the open yard-way? Can I not pass the sheds
And through to the mowie? Only the dead in their beds
Can know the fearful anguish that this is so.

I kiss the stones. I kiss the moss on the wall,
And wish I could pass impregnate into the place.
I wish I could take it all in a last embrace.
I wish with my breast I could crush it, perish it all.

Piano

Softly, in the dusk, a woman is singing to me;
Taking me back down the vista of years, till I see
A child sitting under the piano, in the boom of the tingling strings
And pressing the small, poised feet of a mother who smiles as she
    sings.

In spite of myself, the insidious mastery of song
Betrays me back, till the heart of me weeps to belong
To the old Sunday evenings at home, with winter outside
And hymns in the cosy parlour, the tinkling piano our guide.

So now it is vain for the singer to burst into clamour
With the great black piano appassionato. The glamour
Of childish days is upon me, my manhood is cast
Down in the flood of remembrance, I weep like a child for the past.

Medlars and Sorb-Apples

I love you, rotten.
Delicious rottenness!

I love to suck you out from your skins,
So brown and soft and coming suave,
So morbid, as the Italians say.

What a rare, powerful, reminiscent flavour
Comes out of your falling through the stages of decay,
Stream within stream!

Something of the same flavour as Syracusan muscat wine
Or vulgar Marsala.

Though even the word Marsala will smack of preciosity
Now in the pussy-foot West.

What is it?
What is it in the grape turning raisin,
In the medlar, in the sorb-apple,
Wineskins of brown morbidity,
Autumnal excrementa,
What is it that reminds us of white gods?

Gods, nude as blanched nut-kernels,
Strangely, half-sinisterly flesh-fragrant
As if with sweat,
And drenched with mystery?
Sorb-apples, medlars with dead crowns.

I say, wonderful are the hellish experiences,
Orphic, delicate
Dionysos of the Underworld.

A kiss, and a vivid spasm of farewell, a moment's orgasm of rupture,
Then along the damp road alone, till the next turning.
And there, a new partner, a new parting, a new unfusing into twain,
A new gasp of further isolation,
A new intoxication of loneliness, among decaying frost-cold leaves.

Going down the strange lanes of hell, more and more intensely alone,
The fibres of the heart parting one after the other,
And yet the soul continuing, naked-footed, ever more vividly
     embodied,
Like a flame blown whiter and whiter
In a deeper and deeper darkness,
Ever more exquisite, distilled in separation.

So, in the strange retorts of medlars and sorb-apples
The distilled essence of hell.
The exquisite fragrance of leave-taking. *Jamque vale!*[1]
Orpheus, and the winding, leaf-clogged, silent lanes of Hell.

Each soul departing with its own isolation,
Strangest of all strange companions,
And best.

Medlars, sorb-apples,
More than sweet,
Flux of autumn,
Sucked out of your empty bladders
And sipped down, perhaps, with a sip of Marsala
So that the rambling, sky-dropped grape can add its music to yours,
Orphic farewell, and farewell, and farewell,
And the *ego sum*[2] of Dionysos,
The *sono io*[3] of perfect drunkenness,
Intoxication of final loneliness.

---

[1]*Jamque vale!*] Now farewell!
[2]*ego sum*] I am
[3]*sono io*] O I speak out

AMY LOWELL
(1874–1925)

In a Garden

Gushing from the mouths of stone men
To spread at ease under the sky
In granite-lipped basins,
Where iris dabble their feet
And rustle to a passing wind,
The water fills the garden with its rushing,
In the midst of the quiet of close-clipped lawns.

Damp smell the ferns in tunnels of stone,
Where trickle and plash the fountains,
Marble fountains, yellowed with much water.

Splashing down moss-tarnished steps
It falls, the water;
And the air is throbbing with it;
With its gurgling and running;
With its leaping, and deep, cool murmur.

And I wished for night and you.
I wanted to see you in the swimming-pool,
White and shining in the silver-flecked water.
While the moon rode over the garden,
High in the arch of night,
And the scent of the lilacs was heavy with stillness.

Night and the water, and you in your whiteness, bathing!

Venus Transiens

Tell me,
Was Venus more beautiful
Than you are,
When she topped
The crinkled waves,
Drifting shoreward
On her plaited shell?
Was Botticelli's vision
Fairer than mine;
And were the painted rosebuds
He tossed his lady,
Of better worth
Than the words I blow about you
To cover your too great loveliness
As with a gauze
Of misted silver?

For me,
You stand poised
In the blue and buoyant air,
Cinctured by bright winds,
Treading the sunlight.
And the waves which precede you
Ripple and stir
The sands at my feet.

The Travelling Bear

Grass-blades push up between the cobblestones
And catch the sun on their flat sides
Shooting it back,
Gold and emerald,
Into the eyes of passers-by.

And over the cobblestones,
Square-footed and heavy,
Dances the trained bear.
The cobbles cut his feet,
And he has a ring in his nose

Which hurts him;
But still he dances,
For the keeper pricks him with a sharp stick,
Under his fur.

Now the crowd gapes and chuckles,
And boys and young women shuffle their feet in time to the dancing
      bear.
They see him wobbling
Against a dust of emerald and gold,
And they are greatly delighted.

The legs of the bear shake with fatigue
And his back aches,
And the shining grass-blades dazzle and confuse him.
But still he dances,
Because of the little, pointed stick.

Solitaire

When night drifts along the streets of the city,
And sifts down between the uneven roofs,
My mind begins to peek and peer.
It plays at ball in old, blue Chinese gardens,
And shakes wrought dice-cups in Pagan temples,
Amid the broken flutings of white pillars.
It dances with purple and yellow crocuses in its hair,
And its feet shine as they flutter over drenched grasses.
How light and laughing my mind is,
When all the good folk have put out their bed-room candles,
And the city is still!

Sunshine

The pool is edged with the blade-like leaves of irises.
If I throw a stone into the placid water
It suddenly stiffens
Into rings and rings
Of sharp gold wire.

A Year Passes

Beyond the porcelain fence of the pleasure-garden,
I hear the frogs in the blue-green rice-fields;
But the sword-shaped moon
Has cut my heart in two.

To a Husband

Brighter than fireflies upon the Uji River
Are your words in the dark, Beloved.

The Emperor's Garden

Once, in the sultry heats of Midsummer,
An Emperor caused the miniature mountains in his garden
To be covered with white silk,
That so crowned
They might cool his eyes
With the sparkle of snow.

A Decade

When you came, you were like red wine and honey,
And the taste of you burnt my mouth with its sweetness.
Now you are like morning bread,
Smooth and pleasant.
I hardly taste you at all for I know your savour,
But I am completely nourished.

YONE NOGUCHI
(1875–1947)

I Have Cast the World

I have cast the world,
    and think me as nothing.
Yet I feel cold on snow-falling day,
And happy on flower day.

EZRA POUND
(1885–1972)

Δώρια[1]

Be in me as the eternal moods
    of the bleak wind, and not
As transient things are—
    gaiety of flowers.
Have me in the strong loneliness
    of sunless cliffs
And of grey waters.
    Let the gods speak softly of us
In days hereafter,
    The shadowy flowers of Orcus
Remember Thee.

The Return

See, they return; ah, see the tentative
Movements, and the slow feet,
The trouble in the pace and the uncertain
Wavering!

See, they return, one, and by one,
With fear, as half-awakened;
As if the snow should hesitate
And murmur in the wind
    and half turn back;

---

[1]*Dória*] in the Doric manner, or "things Doric."

These were the "Wing'd-with-Awe,"
     Inviolable.

Gods of the winged shoe!
With them the silver hounds
          sniffing the trace of air!
Haie! Haie!
     These were the swift to harry;
These the keen-scented;
These were the souls of blood.

Slow on the leash,
          pallid the leash-men!

After Ch'u Yuan

I will get me to the wood
Where the gods walk garlanded in wisteria,
By the silver-blue flood move others with ivory cars.
There come forth many maidens
     to gather grapes for the leopards, my friend.
For there are leopards drawing the cars.

I will walk in the glade,
I will come out of the new thicket
     and accost the procession of maidens.

Liu Ch'e

The rustling of the silk is discontinued,
Dust drifts over the courtyard,
There is no sound of footfall, and the leaves
Scurry into heaps and lie still,
And she the rejoicer of the heart is beneath them:

A wet leaf that clings to the threshold.

Fan-Piece for Her Imperial Lord

O fan of white silk,
            clear as frost on the grass-blade,
You also are laid aside.

Couplet

Drawing a sword, cut into water, water again flow:
Raise cup, quench sorrow, sorrow again sorry.

The Garret

Come, let us pity those who are better off than we are.
Come, my friend, and remember
      that the rich have butlers and no friends,
And we have friends and no butlers.
Come, let us pity the married and the unmarried.

Dawn enters with little feet
      like a gilded Pavlova,
And I am near my desire.
Nor has life in it aught better
Than this hour of clear coolness,
      the hour of waking together.

Dance Figure

For the Marriage in Cana of Galilee

Dark eyed,
O woman of my dreams,
Ivory sandaled,
There is none like thee among the dancers,
None with swift feet.

I have not found thee in the tents,
In the broken darkness.
I have not found thee at the well-head
Among the women with pitchers.

Thine arms are as a young sapling under the bark;
Thy face as a river with lights.

White as an almond are thy shoulders;
As new almonds stripped from the husk.

They guard thee not with eunuchs;
Not with bars of copper.

Gilt turquoise and silver are in the place of thy rest.
A brown robe, with threads of gold woven in patterns,
        hast thou gathered about thee,
O Nathat-Ikanaie, "Tree-at-the-river."

As a rillet among the sedge are thy hands upon me;
Thy fingers a frosted stream.

Thy maidens are white like pebbles;
Their music about thee!

There is none like thee among the dancers;
None with swift feet.

April

Nympharum membra disjecta[1]

Three spirits came to me
And drew me apart
To where the olive boughs
Lay stripped upon the ground:
Pale carnage beneath bright mist.

---

[1]*Nympharum membra disjecta*] The scattered limbs of the nymph

Further Instructions

Come, my songs, let us express our baser passions,
Let us express our envy of the man with a steady job and no worry
    about the future.
You are very idle, my songs.
I fear you will come to a bad end.
You stand about in the streets,
You loiter at the corners and bus-stops,
You do next to nothing at all.

You do not even express our inner nobilities,
You will come to a very bad end.

And I?
I have gone half cracked,
I have talked to you so much that
      I almost see you about me,
Insolent little beasts, shameless, devoid of clothing!

But you, newest song of the lot,
You are not old enough to have done much mischief,
I will get you a green coat out of China
With dragons worked upon it,
I will get you the scarlet silk trousers
From the statue of the infant Christ at Santa Maria Novella,
Lest they say we are lacking in taste,
Or that there is no caste in this family.

Το Καλὸν[1]

    Even in my dreams you have denied yourself to me
    And sent me only your handmaids.

---

[1]**Το Καλὸν**] The beautiful

The Coming of War: Actaeon

An image of Lethe,
      and the fields
Full of faint light
      but golden,
Gray cliffs,
      and beneath them
A sea
Harsher than granite,
      unstill, never ceasing;
High forms
      with the movement of gods,
Perilous aspect;
      And one said:
"This is Actaeon."
      Actaeon of golden greaves!
Over fair meadows,
Over the cool face of that field,
Unstill, even moving,
Hosts of an ancient people,
The silent cortège.

Ts'ai Chi'h

The petals fall in the fountain,
      the orange-coloured rose-leaves,
Their ochre clings to the stone.

In a Station of the Metro

The apparition of these faces in the crowd;
Petals on a wet, black bough.

Alba

As cool as the pale wet leaves
                              of lily-of-the-valley
She lay beside me in the dawn.

Image from d'Orleans

Young men riding in the street
In the bright new season
Spur without reason,
Causing their steeds to leap.

And at the pace they keep
Their horses' armoured feet
Strike sparks from the cobbled street
In the bright new season.

Epitaphs

Fu I
Fu I loved the high cloud and the hill,
Alas, he died of alcohol.

Li Po
And Li Po also died drunk.
He tried to embrace a moon
In the Yellow River.

The River-Merchant's Wife: A Letter

Translated from the Chinese of Li Po [Rihaku]

While my hair was still cut straight across my forehead
I played about the front gate, pulling flowers.
You came by on bamboo stilts, playing horse,
You walked about my seat, playing with blue plums.

And we went on living in the village of Chokan:
Two small people, without dislike or suspicion.

At fourteen I married My Lord you.
I never laughed, being bashful.
Lowering my head, I looked at the wall.
Called to, a thousand times, I never looked back.

At fifteen I stopped scowling,
I desired my dust to be mingled with yours
Forever and forever and forever.
Why should I climb the look out?

At sixteen you departed,
You went into far Ku-to-Yen, by the river of swirling eddies,
And you have been gone five months.
The monkeys make sorrowful noise overhead.
You dragged your feet when you went out.
By the gate now, the moss is grown, the different mosses,
Too deep to clear them away!
The leaves fall early this autumn, in wind.
The paired butterflies are already yellow with August
Over the grass in the West garden;
They hurt me.
I grow older.
If you are coming down through the narrows of the river Kiang,
Please let me know beforehand,
And I will come out to meet you
              As far as Cho-fu-Sa.

The Jewel Stairs' Grievance

by Rihaku

The jewelled steps are already quite white with dew,
It is so late that the dew soaks my gauze stockings,
And I let down the crystal curtain
And watch the moon through the clear autumn.

NOTE.—Jewel stairs, therefore a palace. Grievance, therefore there is something to complain of. Gauze stockings, therefore a court lady, not a servant who complains. Clear autumn, therefore he has no excuse on account of weather. Also she has come early, for the dew has not merely whitened the stairs, but has soaked her stockings. The poem is especially prized because she utters no direct reproach.

Exile's Letter

by Rihaku

To So-Kin of Rakuyo, ancient friend, Chancellor of Gen.
Now I remember that you built me a special tavern
By the south side of the bridge at Ten-Shin.
With yellow gold and white jewels, we paid for songs and laughter
And we were drunk for month on month, forgetting the kings and
    princes.
Intelligent men came drifting in from the sea and from the west border,
And with them, and with you especially
There was nothing at cross purpose,
And they made nothing of sea-crossing or of mountain-crossing,
If only they could be of that fellowship,
And we all spoke out our hearts and minds, and without regret.

And then I was sent off to South Wei,
    smothered in laurel groves,
And you to the north of Raku-hoku,
Till we had nothing but thoughts and memories in common.
And then, when separation had come to its worst,
We met, and travelled into Sen-Go,
Through all the thirty-six folds of the turning and twisting waters,
Into a valley of the thousand bright flowers,
That was the first valley;
And into ten thousand valleys full of voices and pine-winds.
And with silver harness and reins of gold,
Out come the East of Kan foreman and his company.
And there came also the "True man" of Shi-yo to meet me,
Playing on a jewelled mouth-organ.
In the storied houses of San-Ko they gave us more Sennin music,
Many instruments, like the sound of young phœnix broods.
The foreman of Kan Chu, drunk, danced
    because his long sleeves wouldn't keep still
With that music playing,
And I, wrapped in brocade, went to sleep with my head on his lap,
And my spirit so high it was all over the heavens,
And before the end of the day we were scattered like stars, or rain.

I had to be off to So, far away over the waters,
You back to your river-bridge.

And your father, who was brave as a leopard,
Was governor in Hei Shu, and put down the barbarian rabble.

And one May he had you send for me,
       despite the long distance.
And what with broken wheels and so on, I won't say it wasn't hard going,
Over roads twisted like sheep's guts.
And I was still going, late in the year,
       in the cutting wind from the North,
And thinking how little you cared for the cost,
       and you caring enough to pay it.
And what a reception:
Red jade cups, food well set on a blue jewelled table,
And I was drunk, and had no thought of returning.
And you would walk out with me to the western corner of the castle,
To the dynastic temple, with water about it clear as blue jade,
With boats floating, and the sound of mouth-organs and drums,
With ripples like dragon-scales, going grass green on the water,
Pleasure lasting, with courtezans, going and coming without
       hindrance,
With the willow flakes falling like snow,
And the vermilioned girls getting drunk about sunset,
And the water a hundred feet deep reflecting green eyebrows
—Eyebrows painted green are a fine sight in young moonlight,
Gracefully painted—
And the girls singing back at each other,
Dancing in transparent brocade,
And the wind lifting the song, and interrupting it,
Tossing it up under the clouds.
       And all this comes to an end.
       And is not again to be met with.
I went up to the court for examination,
Tried Layu's luck, offered the Choyo song,
And got no promotion,
       and went back to the East Mountains white-headed.
And once again, later, we met at the South bridgehead.
And then the crowd broke up, you went north to San palace,
And if you ask how I regret that parting:
       It is like the flowers falling at Spring's end
              Confused, whirled in a tangle.
What is the use of talking, and there is no end of talking,
There is no end of things in the heart.
I call in the boy,
Have him sit on his knees here
       To seal this,
And send it a thousand miles, thinking.

From Rihaku
FOUR POEMS OF DEPARTURE

Light rain is on the light dust
The willows of the inn-yard
Will be going greener and greener,
But you, Sir, had better take wine ere your departure,
For you will have no friends about you
When you come to the gates of Go.

Separation on the River Kiang

Ko-Jin goes west from Ko-kaku-ro,
The smoke-flowers are blurred over the river.
His lone sail blots the far sky.
And now I see only the river,
          The long Kiang, reaching heaven.

Taking Leave of a Friend

Blue mountains to the north of the walls,
White river winding about them;
Here we must make separation
And go out through a thousand miles of dead grass.
Mind like a floating wide cloud,
Sunset like the parting of old acquaintances
Who bow over their clasped hands at a distance.
Our horses neigh to each other
          as we are departing.

Leave-Taking Near Shoku

"Sanso, King of Shoku, built roads"

They say the roads of Sanso are steep,
Sheer as the mountains.
The walls rise in a man's face,

Clouds grow out of the hill
      at his horse's bridle.
Sweet trees are on the paved way of the Shin,
Their trunks burst through the paving,
And freshets are bursting their ice
      in the midst of Shoku, a proud city.

Men's fates are already set,
There is no need of asking diviners.

The City of Choan

The phœnix are at play on their terrace.
The phœnix are gone, the river flows on alone.
Flowers and grass
Cover over the dark path
      where lay the dynastic house of the Go.
The bright cloths and bright caps of Shin
Are now the base of old hills.

The Three Mountains fall through the far heaven,
The isle of White Heron
      splits the two streams apart.
Now the high clouds cover the sun
And I can not see Choan afar
And I am sad.

A Ballad of the Mulberry Road

(Fenollosa MSS., very early)[1]

The sun rises in south east corner of things
To look on the tall house of the Shin
For they have a daughter named Rafu,
      (pretty girl)
She made the name for herself: "Gauze Veil,"

---

[1] Ernest Fenollosa was a scholar of Chinese and Japanese poetry. Fenollosa's widow encouraged Pound to use her husband's notes and glosses of the written characters.

For she feeds mulberries to silkworms,
      She gets them by the south wall of the town.

A place of felicitous meeting.
Riu's house stands out on the sky,
        with glitter of colour
As Butei of Kan had made the high golden lotus
        to gather his dews,
Before it another house which I do not know:
How shall we know all the friends
        whom we met on strange roadways?

To-Em-Mei's "The Unmoving Cloud"

by T'ao Yuan Ming
A.D. 365–427

"Wet springtime," says To-Em-Mei,
"Wet spring in the garden."

I

The clouds have gathered, and gathered,
        and the rain falls and falls,
The eight ply of the heavens
        are all folded into one darkness,
And the wide, flat road stretches out.
I stop in my room toward the East, quiet, quiet,
I pat my new cask of wine.
My friends are estranged, or far distant,
I bow my head and stand still.

II

Rain, rain, and the clouds have gathered,
The eight ply of the heavens are darkness,
The flat land is turned into river.
        "Wine, wine, here is wine!"
I drink by my eastern window.
I think of talking and man,
And no boat, no carriage, approaches.

III

The trees in my east-looking garden
       are bursting out with new twigs,
They try to stir new affection,

And men say the sun and moon keep on moving
       because they can't find a soft seat.

The birds flutter to rest in my tree,
       and I think I have heard them saying,
"It is not that there are no other men
But we like this fellow the best,
But however we long to speak
He can not know of our sorrow."

Chanson Arabe

I have shaken with love half the night.
The winter rain falls in the street.
She is but half my age;
      Whither, whither am I going?
I have shaken with love half the night.
She is but half my age.
      Whither, whither am I going?

Dawn on the Mountain

by Omakitsu

Peach flowers turn the dew crimson,
Green willows melt in the mist,
The servant will not sweep up the fallen petals,
      And the nightingales
Persist in their singing.

WALLACE STEVENS
(1879–1955)

From a Junk

A great fish plunges in the dark,
Its fins of rutted silver; sides,
Belabored with a foamy light;
And back, brilliant with scaly salt.
It glistens in the flapping wind,
Burns there and glistens, wide and wide,
Under the five-horned stars of night,
In wind and wave . . . It is the moon.

Home Again

Back within the valley,
Down from the divide,
No more flaming clouds about,
O! the soft hillside,
And my cottage light,
And the starry night.

The Silver Plough-Boy

A black figure dances in a black field.
It seizes a sheet—from the ground, from a bush—as if spread there by
    some wash-woman for the night.

It wraps the sheet around its body, until the black figure is silver.
It dances down a furrow, in the early light, back of a crazy plough,
    the green blades following.
How soon the silver fades in the dust! How soon the black figure slips
    from the wrinkled sheet. How softly the sheet falls to the ground!

Peter Quince at the Clavier

I

Just as my fingers on these keys
Make music, so the self-same sounds
On my spirit make a music too.

Music is feeling then, not sound;
And thus it is that what I feel,
Here in this room, desiring you,

Thinking of your blue-shadowed silk,
Is music. It is like the strain
Waked in the elders by Susanna:

Of a green evening, clear and warm,
She bathed in her still garden, while
The red-eyed elders, watching, felt

The basses of their being throb
In witching chords, and their thin blood
Pulse pizzicati of Hosanna.

II

In the green water, clear and warm,
Susanna lay.
She searched
The touch of springs,
And found
Concealed imaginings.
She sighed
For so much melody.

Upon the bank she stood
In the cool
Of spent emotions.
She felt, among the leaves,

The dew
Of old devotions.

She walked upon the grass,
Still quavering.
The winds were like her maids,
On timid feet,
Fetching her woven scarves,
Yet wavering.

A breath upon her hand
Muted the night.
She turned—
A cymbal crashed,
And roaring horns.

III

Soon, with a noise like tambourines,
Came her attendant Byzantines.

They wondered why Susanna cried
Against the elders by her side:

And as they whispered, the refrain
Was like a willow swept by rain.

Anon, their lamps' uplifted flame
Revealed Susanna and her shame.

And then the simpering Byzantines,
Fled, with a noise like tambourines.

IV

Beauty is momentary in the mind—
The fitful tracing of a portal;
But in the flesh it is immortal.

The body dies; the body's beauty lives.
So evenings die, in their green going,
A wave, interminably flowing.
So gardens die, their meek breath scenting
The cowl of Winter, done repenting.
So maidens die, to the auroral
Celebration of a maiden's choral.

Susanna's music touched the bawdy strings
Of those white elders; but, escaping,

Left only Death's ironic scraping.
Now, in its immortality, it plays
On the clear viol of her memory,
And makes a constant sacrament of praise.

Sunday Morning

I

Complacencies of the peignoir, and late
Coffee and oranges in a sunny chair,
And the green freedom of a cockatoo
Upon a rug, mingle to dissipate
The holy hush of ancient sacrifice.
She dreams a little, and she feels the dark
Encroachment of that old catastrophe,
As a calm darkens among water-lights.
The pungent oranges and bright, green wings
Seem things in some procession of the dead,
Winding across wide water, without sound.
The day is like wide water, without sound,
Stilled for the passing of her dreaming feet
Over the seas, to silent Palestine,
Dominion of the blood and sepulchre.

II

She hears, upon that water without sound,
A voice that cries: "The tomb in Palestine
Is not the porch of spirits lingering;
It is the grave of Jesus, where he lay."
We live in an old chaos of the sun,
Or old dependency of day and night,
Or island solitude, unsponsored, free,
Of that wide water, inescapable.
Deer walk upon our mountains, and the quail
Whistle about us their spontaneous cries;
Sweet berries ripen in the wilderness;
And, in the isolation of the sky,
At evening, casual flocks of pigeons make
Ambiguous undulations as they sink,
Downward to darkness, on extended wings.

III

She says: "I am content when wakened birds,
Before they fly, test the reality
Of misty fields, by their sweet questionings;
But when the birds are gone, and their warm fields
Return no more, where, then, is paradise?"
There is not any haunt of prophecy,
Nor any old chimera of the grave,
Neither the golden underground, nor isle
Melodious, where spirits gat them home,
Nor visionary South, nor cloudy palm
Remote on heaven's hill, that has endured
As April's green endures; or will endure
Like her remembrance of awakened birds,
Or her desire for June and evening, tipped
By the consummation of the swallow's wings.

IV

She says, "But in contentment I still feel
The need of some imperishable bliss."
Death is the mother of beauty; hence from her,
Alone, shall come fulfilment to our dreams
And our desires. Although she strews the leaves
Of sure obliteration on our paths—
The path sick sorrow took, the many paths
Where triumph rang its brassy phrase, or love
Whispered a little out of tenderness—
She makes the willow shiver in the sun
For maidens who were wont to sit and gaze
Upon the grass, relinquished to their feet.
She causes boys to bring sweet-smelling pears
And plums in ponderous piles. The maidens taste
And stray impassioned in the littering leaves.

V

Supple and turbulent, a ring of men
Shall chant in orgy on a summer morn
Their boisterous devotion to the sun—
Not as a god, but as a god might be,
Naked among them, like a savage source.
Their chant shall be a chant of paradise,
Out of their blood, returning to the sky;

And in their chant shall enter, voice by voice,
The windy lake wherein their lord delights,
The trees, like seraphim, and echoing hills,
That choir among themselves long afterward.
They shall know well the heavenly fellowship
Of men that perish and of summer morn—
And whence they came and whither they shall go,
The dew upon their feet shall manifest.

Primordia

In the Northwest

1

All over Minnesota,
Cerise sopranos,
Walking in the snow,
Answer, humming,
The male voice of the wind in the dry leaves
Of the lake-hollows.
For one,
The syllables of the gulls and of the crows
And of the blue-bird
Meet in the name
Of Jalmar Lillygreen.
There is his motion
In the flowing of black water.

2

The child's hair is of the color of the hay in the haystack, around which the four black horses stand.
There is the same color in the bellies of frogs, in clays, withered reeds, skins, wood, sunlight.

3

The blunt ice flows down the Mississippi,
At night.
In the morning, the clear river
Is full of reflections,
Beautiful alliterations of shadows and of things shadowed.

4

The horses gnaw the bark from the trees.
The horses are hollow,
The trunks of the trees are hollow.
Why do the horses have eyes and ears?
The trees do not.
Why can the horses move about on the ground?
The trees cannot.
The horses weary themselves hunting for green grass.
The trees stand still,
The trees drink.
The water runs away from the horses,
La, la, la, la, la, la, la, la,
Dee, dum, diddle, dee, dee, diddle, dee, da.

5

The birch trees draw up whiteness from the ground.
In the swamps, bushes draw up dark red,
Or yellow.
O, boatman,
What are you drawing from the rain-pointed water?
O, boatman,
What you are drawing from the rain-pointed water?
Are you two boatmen
Different from each other?

In the South

6

Unctuous furrows,
The ploughman portrays in you
The spring about him:
Compilation of the effects
Of magenta blooming in the Judas-tree
And of purple blooming in the eucalyptus—
Map of yesterday's earth
And of to-morrow's heaven.

7

The lilacs wither in the Carolinas.
Already the butterflies flutter above the cabins.
Already the new-born children interpret love
In the voices of mothers.

Timeless mother,
How is it that your aspic nipples
For once vent honey?

The pine-tree sweetens my body,
The white iris beautifies me.

8

The black mother of eleven children
Hangs her quilt under the pine-trees.
There is a connection between the colors,
The shapes of the patches,
And the eleven children . . .
Frail princes of distant Monaco,
That paragon of a parasol
Discloses
At least one baby in you.

9

The trade-wind jingles the rings in the nets around the racks by the
     docks on Indian River.
It is the same jingle of the water among the roots under the banks of
     the palmettoes,
It is the same jingle of the red-bird breasting the orange-trees out of
     the cedars.
Yet there is no spring in Florida, neither in boskage perdu, nor on the
     nunnery beaches.

Valley Candle

My candle burned alone in an immense valley.
Beams of the huge night converged upon it,
Until the wind blew.
Then beams of the huge night
Converged upon its image,
Until the wind blew.

Thirteen Ways of Looking at a Blackbird

I

Among twenty snowy mountains,
The only moving thing
Was the eye of the blackbird.

II

I was of three minds,
Like a tree
In which there are three blackbirds.

III

The blackbird whirled in the autumn winds,
It was a small part of the pantomime.

IV

A man and a woman
Are one.
A man and a woman and a blackbird
Are one.

V

I do not know which to prefer—
The beauty of inflections
Or the beauty of innuendoes,
The blackbird whistling
Or just after.

VI

Icicles filled the long window
With barbaric glass.
The shadow of the blackbird
Crossed it, to and fro.
The mood
Traced in the shadow
An indecipherable cause.

VII

O thin men of Haddam,
Why do you imagine golden birds?
Do you not see how the blackbird

Walks around the feet
Of the women about you?

VIII

I know noble accents
And lucid, inescapable rhythms;
But I know, too,
That the blackbird is involved
In what I know.

IX

When the blackbird flew out of sight,
It marked the edge
Of one of many circles.

X

At the sight of blackbirds
Flying in a green light,
Even the bawds of euphony
Would cry out sharply.

XI

He rode over Connecticut
In a glass coach.
Once, a fear pierced him,
In that he mistook
The shadow of his equipage
For blackbirds.

XII

The river is moving.
The blackbird must be flying.

XIII

It was evening all afternoon.
It was snowing
And it was going to snow.
The blackbird sat
In the cedar-limbs.

Metaphors of a Magnifico

Twenty men crossing a bridge,
Into a village,
Are twenty men crossing twenty bridges,
Into twenty villages,
Or one man
Crossing a single bridge into a village.

This is old song
That will not declare itself . . .

Twenty men crossing a bridge,
Into a village,
Are
Twenty men crossing a bridge
Into a village.

That will not declare itself
Yet is certain as meaning . . .

The boots of the men clump
On the boards of the bridge.
The first white wall of the village
Rises through fruit-trees.

Of what was it I was thinking?

So the meaning escapes.

The first white wall of the village . . .
The fruit-trees . . .

Architecture for the Adoration of Beauty

I

What manner of building shall we build for
the adoration of beauty?
Let us design this chastel de chasteté,
De pensée . . .
Never cease to deploy the structure . . .
Keep the laborers shouldering plinths . . .
Pass the whole of life earing the clink of the
chisels of the stone-cutters cutting the stones . . .

II

In this house, what manner of utterance shall
there be?
What heavenly dithyramb
And cantilene?
What niggling forms of gargoyle patter?
Of what shall the speech be,
In that splay of marble
And of obedient pillars?

III

And how shall those come vested that come there?
In their ugly reminders?
Or gaudy as tulips?
As they climb the stairs
To the group of Flora Coddling Hecuba?
As they climb the flights
To the closes
Overlooking whole seasons?

IV

Let us build the building of light.
Push up the towers
To the cock-tops.
These are the pointings of our edifice,
Which, like a gorgeous palm,
Shall tuft the commonplace.
These are the window-sill
On which the quiet moonlight lies.

V

How shall we hew the sun,
Split it and make blocks,
To build a ruddy palace?
How carve the violet moon
To set in nicks?
Let us fix portals, East and West,
Abhorring green-blue North and blue-green South.
Our chiefest dome a demoiselle of gold.
Pierce the interior with pouring shafts,
In diverse chambers.
Pierce, too, with buttresses of coral air

And purple timbers,
Various argentines,
Embossings of the sky.

Fabliau of Florida

Barque of phosphor
On the palmy beach,

Move outward into heaven,
Into the alabasters
And night blues.

Foam and cloud are one.
Sultry moon-monsters
Are dissolving.

Fill your black hull
With white moonlight.

There will never be an end
To this droning of the surf.

The Load of Sugar-Cane

The going of the glade-boat
Is like water flowing;

Like water flowing
Through the green saw-grass,
Under the rainbows;

Under the rainbows
That are like birds,
Turning, bedizened,

While the wind still whistles
As kildeer do,

When they rise
At the red turban
Of the boatman.

Hibiscus on the Sleeping Shores

I say now, Fernando, that on that day
The mind roamed as a moth roams,
Among the blooms beyond the open sand;

And that whatever noise the motion of the waves
Made on the sea-weeds and the covered stones
Disturbed not even the most idle ear.

Then it was that that monstered moth
Which had lain folded against the blue
And the colored purple of the lazy sea,

And which had drowsed along the bony shores,
Shut to the blather that the water made,
Rose up besprent and sought the flaming red

Dabbled with yellow pollen—red as red
As the flag above the old café—
And roamed there all the stupid afternoon.

The Bird with the Coppery, Keen Claws

Above the forest of the parakeets,
A parakeet of parakeets prevails,
A pip of life amid a mort of tails.

(The rudiments of tropics are around,
Aloe of ivory, pear of rusty rind).
His lids are white because his eyes are blind.

He is not paradise of parakeets,
Of his gold ether, golden alguazil,
Except because he broods there and is still.

Panache upon panache, his tails deploy
Upward and outward, in green-vented forms,
His tip a drop of water full of storms.

But though the turbulent tinges undulate
As his pure intellect applies its laws,
He moves not on his coppery, keen claws.

He munches a dry shell while he exerts
His will, yet never ceases, perfect cock,
To flare, in the sun-pallor of his rock.

O, Florida, Venereal Soil

A few things for themselves,
Convolvulus and coral,
Buzzards and live-moss,
Tiestas from the keys,
A few things for themselves,
Florida, venereal soil,
Disclose to the lover.

The dreadful sundry of this world,
The Cuban, Polodowsky,
The Mexican women,
The negro undertaker
Killing the time between corpses
Fishing for crawfish . . .
Virgin of boorish births,

Swiftly in the nights,
In the porches of Key West,
Behind the bougainvilleas,
After the guitar is asleep,
Lasciviously as the wind,
You come tormenting,
Insatiable,

When you might sit,
A scholar of darkness,
Sequestered over the sea,
Wearing a clear tiara
Of red and blue and red,
Sparkling, solitary, still,
In the high sea-shadow.

Donna, donna, dark,
Stooping in indigo gown
And cloudy constellations,
Conceal yourself or disclose
Fewest things to the lover—
A hand that bears a thick-leaved fruit,
A pungent bloom against your shade.

WILLIAM CARLOS WILLIAMS
(1883–1963)

Contemporania

The corner of a great rain
Steamy with the country
Has fallen upon my garden.

I go back and forth now
And the little leaves follow me
Talking of the great rain,
Of branches broken,
And the farmer's curses!

But I go back and forth
In this corner of a garden
And the green shoots follow me
Praising the great rain.

We are not curst together,
The leaves and I,
Framing devices, flower devices
And other ways of peopling
The barren country.

Truly it was a very great rain
That makes the little leaves follow me.

Offering

As the hedges, clipt and even,
That parallel the common way—
And upon one side the hedges
And upon one side bare trees—
As these hedges bear the dried leaves
That have fallen from spent branches,—
Having caught them in mid air—
And hold them yet awhile
That they may not be so soon
Jostled about and tramped on—

The red, the yellow, the purple—blues—
So do my words catch and bear
Both leaves and flowers that are fallen—
In all places before the feet
Of the passing many—to bear them
Yet awhile before they are trodden.

Postlude

Now that I have cooled to you
Let there be gold of tarnished masonry,
Temples soothed by the sun to ruin
That sleep utterly.
Give me hand for the dances,
Ripples at Philæ, in and out,
And lips, my Lesbian,
Wall flowers that once were flame.

Your hair is my Carthage
And my arms the bow
And our words arrows
To shoot the stars,
Who from that misty sea
Swarm to destroy us.
But you're there beside me
Oh, how shall I defy you
Who wound me in the night
With breasts shining

Like Venus and like Mars?
The night that is shouting Jason
When the loud eaves rattle
As with waves above me
Blue at the prow of my desire!
O prayers in the dark!
O incense to Poseidon!
Calm in Atlantis.

Marriage

So different, this man
And this woman:
A stream flowing
In a field.

The Young Housewife

At ten A.M. the young housewife
moves about in négligé behind
the wooden walls of her husband's house.
I pass solitary in my car.

Then again she comes to the curb
to call the ice-man, fish-man, and stands
shy, uncorseted, tucking in
stray ends of hair, and I compare her
to a fallen leaf.

The noiseless wheels of my car
rush with a crackling sound over
dried leaves as I bow and pass smiling.

The Shadow

Soft as the bed in the earth
Where a stone has lain—
So soft, so smooth and so cool,

Spring closes me in
With her arms and her hands.

Rich as the smell
Of new earth on a stone,
That has lain, breathing
The damp through its pores—
Spring closes me in
With her blossomy hair;
Brings dark to my eyes.

Metric Figure

There is a bird in the poplars—
It is the sun!
The leaves are little yellow fish
Swimming in the river;
The bird skims above them—
Day is on his wings.
Phoenix!
It is he that is making
The great gleam among the poplars.
It is his singing
Outshines the noise
Of leaves clashing in the wind.

Pastoral

When I was younger
it was plain to me
I must make something of myself.
Older now
I walk back streets
admiring the houses
of the very poor:
roof out of line with sides
the yards cluttered
with old chicken wire, ashes,
furniture gone wrong;

the fences and outhouses
built of barrel-staves
and parts of boxes, all,
if I am fortunate,
smeared a bluish green
that properly weathered
pleases me best
of all colors.

No one
will believe this
of vast import to the nation.

Tract

I will teach you my townspeople
how to perform a funeral —
for you have it over a troop
of artists —
unless one should scour the world —
you have the ground sense necessary.

See! the hearse leads.
I begin with a design for a hearse.
For Christ's sake not black —
nor white either — and not polished!
Let it be weathered — like a farm wagon —
with gilt wheels (this could be
applied fresh at small expense)
or no wheels at all:
a rough dray to drag over the ground.

Knock the glass out!
My God — glass, my townspeople!
For what purpose? Is it for the dead
to look out or for us to see
how well he is housed or to see
the flowers or the lack of them —
or what?
To keep the rain and snow from him?
He will have a heavier rain soon:
pebbles and dirt and what not.

Let there be no glass—
and no upholstery phew!
and no little brass rollers
and small easy wheels on the bottom—
my townspeople what are you thinking of?

A rough plain hearse then
with gilt wheels and no top at all.
On this the coffin lies
by its own weight.

                    No wreathes please—
especially no hot house flowers.
Some common memento is better,
something he prized and is known by:
his old clothes— a few books perhaps—
God knows what! You realize
how we are about these things
my townspeople—
something will be found— anything
even flowers if he had come to that.

So much for the hearse.
For heaven's sake though see to the driver!
Take off the silk hat! In fact
that's no place at all for him—
up there unceremoniously
dragging our friend out to his own dignity!
Bring him down— bring him down!
Low and inconspicuous! I'd not have him ride
on the wagon at all— damn him—
the undertaker's understrapper!
Let him hold the reins
and walk at the side
and inconspicuously too!

Then briefly as to yourselves:
Walk behind— as they do in France,
seventh class, or if you ride
Hell take curtains! Go with some show
of inconvenience; sit openly—
to the weather as to grief.
Or do you think you can shut grief in?
What—from us? We who have perhaps
nothing to lose? Share with us

share with us— it will be money
in your pockets.
                    Go now
I think you are ready.

Promenade

I

Well, mind, here we have
our little son beside us:
a little diversion before breakfast!

Come, we'll walk down the road
till the bacon will be frying.
We might better be idle?
A poem might come of it?
Oh, be useful. Save annoyance
to Flossie and besides—the wind!
It's cold. It blows our
old pants out! It makes us shiver!
See the heavy trees
shifting their weight before it.
Let us be trees, an old house,
a hill with grass on it!
The baby's arms are blue.
Come, move! Be quieted!

II

So. We'll sit here now
and throw pebbles into
this water-trickle.

                    Splash the water up!
(Splash it up, Sonny!) Laugh!
Hit it there deep under the grass.
See it splash! Ah, mind,
see it splash! It is alive!
Throw pieces of broken leaves
into it. They'll pass through.
No! Yes—just!

Away now for the cows! But—
It's cold!
It's getting dark.
It's going to rain.
No further!

III

Oh then, a wreath! Let's
refresh something they
used to write well of.

Two fern plumes. Strip them
to the mid-rib along one side.
Bind the tips with a grass stem.
Bend and intertwist the stalks
at the back. So!
Ah! now we are crowned!
Now we are a poet!

Quickly!
A bunch of little flowers
for Flossie—the little ones
only:
            a red clover, one
blue heal-all, a sprig of
bone-set, one primrose,
a head of Indian tobacco, this
magenta speck and this
little lavender!
                Home now, my mind!—
Sonny's arms are icy, I tell you—
and have breakfast!

Dawn

Ecstatic bird songs pound
the hollow vastness of the sky
with metallic clinkings—
beating color up into it
at a far edge,—beating it, beating it
with rising, triumphant ardor,—
stirring it into warmth,

quickening in it a spreading change,—
bursting wildly against it as
dividing the horizon, a heavy sun
lifts himself—is lifted—
bit by bit above the edge
of things,—runs free at last
out into the open—! lumbering
glorified in full release upward—
                              songs cease.

Good Night

In brilliant gas light
I turn the kitchen spigot
and watch the water plash
into the clean white sink.
On the grooved drain-board
to one side is
a glass filled with parsley—
crisped green.
                    Waiting
for the water to freshen—
I glance at the spotless floor—:
a pair of rubber sandals
lie side by side
under the wall-table,
all is in order for the night.

Waiting, with a glass in my hand
—three girls in crimson satin
pass close before me on
the murmurous background of
the crowded opera—
                        it is
memory playing the clown—
three vague, meaningless girls
full of smells and
the rustling sound of
cloth rubbing on cloth and
little slippers on carpet—
high-school French
spoken in a loud voice!

Parsley in a glass,
still and shining,
brings me back. I take my drink
and yawn deliciously.
I am ready for bed.

Smell!

Oh strong ridged and deeply hollowed
nose of mine! what will you not be smelling?
What tactless asses we are, you and I, boney nose,
always indiscriminate, always unashamed,
and now it is the souring flowers of the bedraggled
poplars: a festering pulp on the wet earth
beneath them. With what deep thirst
we quicken our desires
to that rank odor of a passing spring-time!
Can you not be decent? Can you not reserve your ardors
for something less unlovely? What girl will care
for us, do you think, if we continue in these ways?
Must you taste everything? Must you know everything?
Must you have a part in everything?

Spring Strains

In a tissue-thin monotone of blue-grey buds
crowded erect with desire against
the sky—
             tense blue-grey twigs
slenderly anchoring them down, drawing
them in—
             two blue-grey birds chasing
a third struggle in circles, angles,
swift convergings to a point that bursts
instantly!
             Vibrant bowing limbs
pull downward, sucking in the sky
that bulges from behind, plastering itself

against them in packed rifts, rock blue
and dirty orange!
          But—
(Hold hard, rigid jointed trees!)
the blinding and red-edged sun-blur—
creeping energy, concentrated
counterforce—welds sky, buds, trees,
rivets them in one puckering hold!
Sticks through! Pulls the whole
counter-pulling mass upward, to the right,
locks even the opaque, not yet defined
ground in a terrific drag that is
loosening the very tap-roots!

On a tissue-thin monotone of blue-grey buds
two blue-grey birds, chasing a third,
at full cry! Now they are
flung outward and up—disappearing suddenly!

To a Solitary Disciple

Rather notice, mon cher,
that the moon is
tilted above
the point of the steeple
than that its color
is shell-pink.

Rather observe
that it is early morning
than that the sky
is smooth
as a turquoise.

Rather grasp
how the dark
converging lines
of the steeple
meet at the pinnacle—
perceive how
its little ornament
tries to stop them—

See how it fails!
See how the converging lines
of the hexagonal spire
escape upward—
receding, dividing!
—sepals
that guard and contain
the flower!

Observe
how motionless
the eaten moon
lies in the protecting lines.

It is true:
in the light colors
of morning
brown-stone and slate
shine orange and dark blue.

But observe
the oppressive weight
of the squat edifice!
Observe
the jasmine lightness
of the moon.

Spring Storm

The sky has given over
its bitterness.
Out of the dark change
all day long
rain falls and falls
as if it would never end.
Still the snow keeps
its hold on the ground.
But water, water is seething
from a thousand runnels.
It collects swiftly,
dappled with black
cuts a way for itself

through green ice in the gutters.
Drop after drop it falls
from the withered grass stems
of the overhanging embankment.

Willow Poem

It is a willow when summer is over,
a willow by the river
from which no leaf has fallen nor
bitten by the sun
turned orange or crimson.
The leaves cling and grow paler,
swing and grow paler
over the swirling waters of the river
as if loath to let go,
they are so cool, so drunk with
the swirl of the wind and of the river—
oblivious to winter,
the last to let go and fall
into the water and on the ground.

Blizzard

Snow:
years of anger following
hours that float idly down—
the blizzard
drifts its weight
deeper and deeper for three days
or sixty years, eh? Then
the sun! a clutter of
yellow and blue flakes—
Hairy looking trees stand out
in long alleys
over a wild solitude.
The man turns and there—
his solitary track stretched out
upon the world.

To Waken an Old Lady

Old age is
a flight of small
cheeping birds
skimming
bare trees
above a snow glaze.
Gaining and failing
they are buffetted
by a dark wind—
But what?
On harsh weedstalks
the flock has rested,
the snow
is covered with broken
seedhusks
and the wind tempered
by a shrill
piping of plenty.

Daisy

The dayseye hugging the earth
in August, ha! Spring is
gone down in purple,
weeds stand high in the corn,
the rainbeaten furrow
is clotted with sorrel
and crabgrass, the
branch is black under
the heavy mass of the leaves—
The sun is upon a
slender green stem
ribbed lengthwise.
He lies on his back—
it is a woman also—
he regards his former
majesty and
round the yellow center,

split and creviced and done into
minute flowerheads, he sends out
his twenty rays—a little
and the wind is among them
to grow cool there!

One turns the thing over
in his hand and looks
at it from the rear: brownedged,
green and pointed scales
armor his yellow.
But turn and turn,
the crisp petals remain
brief, translucent, greenfastened,
barely touching at the edges:
blades of limpid seashell.

Waiting

When I am alone I am happy.
The air is cool. The sky is
flecked and splashed and wound
with color. The crimson phalloi
of the sassafrass leaves
hang crowded before me
in shoals on the heavy branches.
When I reach my doorstep
I am greeted by
the happy shrieks of my children
and my heart sinks.
I am crushed.

Are not my children as dear to me
as falling leaves or
must one become stupid
to grow older?
It seems much as if Sorrow
had tripped up my heels.
Let us see, let us see!
What did I plan to say to her
when it should happen to me
as it has happened now?

The Thinker

My wife's new pink slippers
have gay pom-poms.
There is not a spot or a stain
on their satin toes or their sides.
All night they lie together
under her bed's edge.
Shivering I catch sight of them
and smile, in the morning.
Later I watch them
descending the stair,
hurrying through the doors
and round the table,
moving stiffly
with a shake of their gay pom-poms!
And I talk to them
in my secret mind
out of pure happiness.

The Disputants

Upon the table in their bowl
in violent disarray
of yellow sprays, green spikes
of leaves, red pointed petals
and curled heads of blue
and white among the litter
of the forks and crumbs and plates
the flowers remain composed.
Cooly their colloquy continues
above the coffee and loud talk
grown frail as vaudeville.

The Tulip Bed

The May sun—whom
all things imitate—
that glues small leaves to
the wooden trees
shone from the sky
through bluegauze clouds
upon the ground.
Under the leafy trees
where the suburban streets
lay crossed,
with houses on each corner,
tangled shadows had begun
to join
the roadway and the lawns.
With excellent precision
the tulip bed
inside the iron fence
upreared its gaudy
yellow, white and red,
rimmed round with grass,
reposedly.

Blueflags

I stopped the car
to let the children down
where the streets end
in the sun
at the marsh edge
and the reeds begin
and there are small houses
facing the reeds
and the blue mist
in the distance
with grapevine trellises

with grape clusters
small as strawberries
on the vines
and ditches
running springwater
that continue the gutters
with willows over them.
The reeds begin
like water at a shore
their pointed petals waving
dark green and light.
But blueflags are blossoming
in the reeds
which the children pluck
chattering in the reeds
high over their heads
which they part
with bare arms to appear
with fists of flowers
till in the air
there comes the smell
of calamus
from wet, gummy stalks.

The Widow's Lament in Springtime

Sorrow is my own yard
where the new grass
flames as it has flamed
often before but not
with the cold fire
that closes round me this year.
Thirtyfive years
I lived with my husband.
The plumtree is white today
with masses of flowers.

Masses of flowers
load the cherry branches
and color some bushes
yellow and some red
but the grief in my heart
is stronger than they
for though they were my joy
formerly, today I notice them
and turn away forgetting.
Today my son told me
that in the meadows,
at the edge of the heavy woods
in the distance, he saw
trees of white flowers.
I feel that I would like
to go there
and fall into those flowers
and sink into the marsh near them.

The Lonely Street

School is over. It is too hot
to walk at ease. At ease
in light frocks they walk the streets
to while the time away.
They have grown tall. They hold
pink flames in their right hands.
In white from head to foot,
with sidelong, idle look—
in yellow, floating stuff,
black sash and stockings—
touching their avid mouths
with pink sugar on a stick—
like a carnation each holds in her hand—
they mount the lonely street.

The Great Figure

Among the rain
and lights
I saw the figure 5
in gold
on a red
firetruck
moving
with weight and urgency
tense
unheeded
to gong clangs
siren howls
and wheels rumbling
through the dark city.

The Bull

It is in captivity—
ringed, haltered, chained
to a drag—
the bull is godlike

Unlike the cows
he lives alone, nozzles
the sweet grass gingerly
to pass the time away

He kneels, lies down
and stretching out
a foreleg licks himself
about the hoof

then stays
with halfclosed eyes:
Olympian commentary on
the bright passage of days.

   —The great sun
smooths his lacquer
through
the glossy pinetrees

his substance hard
as ivory or glass—
through which the wind
yet plays—
         Milkless
he nods
the hair between his horns
and eyes matted
with hyacinthine curls.

Alphabetical List of Titles and First Lines

Titles are given, in italics, only when distinct from the first lines.

DOVER·THRIFT·EDITIONS

All books complete and unabridged. All 5³⁄₁₆" x 8¹⁄₄," paperbound.
Just $1.00–$2.00 in U.S.A.

A selection of the more than 200 titles in the series.

POETRY

AFRICAN-AMERICAN POETRY: An Anthology, 1773–1930, Joan R. Sherman (ed.). 96pp. 29604-0 $1.00

SELECTED POEMS, Paul Laurence Dunbar. 80pp. 29980-5 $1.00

BEST POEMS OF THE BRONTË SISTERS (ed. by Candace Ward), Emily, Anne and Charlotte Brontë. 64pp. 29529-X $1.00

GREAT POEMS BY AMERICAN WOMEN: An Anthology, Susan L. Rattiner (ed.). 224pp. (Available in U.S. only) 40164-2 $2.00

"GOD'S GRANDEUR" AND OTHER POEMS, Gerard Manley Hopkins. 80pp. 28729-7 $1.00

THE CONCORD HYMN AND OTHER POEMS, Ralph Waldo Emerson. 64pp. 29059-X $1.00

DOVER BEACH AND OTHER POEMS, Matthew Arnold. 112pp. 28037-3 $1.50

HARDY'S SELECTED POEMS, Thomas Hardy. 80pp. 28753-X $1.50

BHAGAVADGITA, Bhagavadgita. 112pp. 27782-8 $1.50

SONGS OF INNOCENCE AND SONGS OF EXPERIENCE, William Blake. 64pp. 27051-3 $1.00

BLAKE'S SELECTED POEMS, William Blake. 96pp. 28517-0 $1.00

THE CLASSIC TRADITION OF HAIKU: An Anthology, Faubion Bowers (ed.). 96pp. 29274-6 $1.50

AENEID, Vergil (Publius Vergilius Maro). 256pp. 28749-1 $2.00

SONNETS FROM THE PORTUGUESE AND OTHER POEMS, Elizabeth Barrett Browning. 64pp. 27052-1 $1.00

MY LAST DUCHESS AND OTHER POEMS, Robert Browning. 128pp. 27783-6 $1.00

POEMS AND SONGS, Robert Burns. 96pp. 26863-2 $1.00

SELECTED POEMS, George Gordon, Lord Byron. 112pp. 27784-4 $1.50

SELECTED POEMS FROM "FLOWERS OF EVIL," Charles Baudelaire. 64pp. 28450-6 $1.00

THE RIME OF THE ANCIENT MARINER AND OTHER POEMS, Samuel Taylor Coleridge. 80pp. 27266-4 $1.00

SELECTED POEMS, Emily Dickinson. 64pp. 26466-1 $1.00

SELECTED POEMS, John Donne. 96pp. 27788-7 $1.50

THE RUBÁIYÁT OF OMAR KHAYYÁM: FIRST AND FIFTH EDITIONS, Edward FitzGerald. 64pp. 26467-X $1.00

A BOY'S WILL AND NORTH OF BOSTON, Robert Frost. 112pp. (Available in U.S. only) 26866-7 $1.00

THE ROAD NOT TAKEN AND OTHER POEMS, Robert Frost. 64pp. (Available in U.S. only) 27550-7 $1.00

A SHROPSHIRE LAD, A. E. Housman. 64pp. 26468-8 $1.00

"LORD RANDAL" AND OTHER BRITISH BALLADS, Francis James Child (ed.). 64pp. 28987-7 $1.00

"TO HIS COY MISTRESS" AND OTHER POEMS, Andrew Marvell. 64pp. 29544-3 $1.00

LYRIC POEMS, John Keats. 80pp. 26871-3 $1.00

THE BOOK OF PSALMS, King James Bible. 128pp. 27541-8 $1.50

GUNGA DIN AND OTHER FAVORITE POEMS, Rudyard Kipling. 80pp. 26471-8 $1.00

THE CONGO AND OTHER POEMS, Vachel Lindsay. 96pp. 27272-9 $1.00

FAVORITE POEMS, Henry Wadsworth Longfellow. 96pp. 27273-7 $1.00

SPOON RIVER ANTHOLOGY, Edgar Lee Masters. 144pp. 27275-3 $1.50

DOVER · THRIFT · EDITIONS

POETRY

"MINIVER CHEEVY" AND OTHER POEMS, Edwin Arlington Robinson. 64pp. 28756-4 $1.00

EARLY POEMS, Ezra Pound. 80pp. (Available in U.S. only) 28745-9 $1.00

EARLY POEMS, William Carlos Williams. 64pp. (Available in U.S. only) 29294-0 $1.00

"THE WASTE LAND" AND OTHER POEMS, T. S. Eliot. 64pp. (Available in U.S. only) 40061-1 $1.00

RENASCENCE AND OTHER POEMS, Edna St. Vincent Millay. 64pp. (Available in U.S. only) 26873-X $1.00

SELECTED POEMS, John Milton. 128pp. 27554-X $1.50

SELECTED CANTERBURY TALES, Geoffrey Chaucer. 144pp. 28241-4 $1.00

GREAT SONNETS, Paul Negri (ed.). 96pp. 28052-7 $1.00

CIVIL WAR POETRY: An Anthology, Paul Negri. 128pp. 29883-3 $1.50

WAR IS KIND AND OTHER POEMS, Stephen Crane. 64pp. 40424-2 $1.00

THE RAVEN AND OTHER FAVORITE POEMS, Edgar Allan Poe. 64pp. 26685-0 $1.00

ESSAY ON MAN AND OTHER POEMS, Alexander Pope. 128pp. 28053-5 $1.50

GOBLIN MARKET AND OTHER POEMS, Christina Rossetti. 64pp. 28055-1 $1.00

CHICAGO POEMS, Carl Sandburg. 80pp. 28057-8 $1.00

THE SHOOTING OF DAN MCGREW AND OTHER POEMS, Robert Service. 96pp. (Available in U.S. only) 27556-6 $1.00

COMPLETE SONNETS, William Shakespeare. 80pp. 26686-9 $1.00

SELECTED POEMS, Percy Bysshe Shelley. 128pp. 27558-2 $1.50

100 BEST-LOVED POEMS, Philip Smith (ed.). 96pp. 28553-7 $1.00

101 GREAT AMERICAN POEMS, The American Poetry & Literacy Project (ed.). (Available in U.S. only) 40158-8 $1.00

NATIVE AMERICAN SONGS AND POEMS: An Anthology, Brian Swann (ed.). 64pp. 29450-1 $1.00

SELECTED POEMS, Alfred Lord Tennyson. 112pp. 27282-6 $1.00

LITTLE ORPHANT ANNIE AND OTHER POEMS, James Whitcomb Riley. 80pp. 28260-0 $1.00

CHRISTMAS CAROLS: COMPLETE VERSES, Shane Weller (ed.). 64pp. 27397-0 $1.00

GREAT LOVE POEMS, Shane Weller (ed.). 128pp. 27284-2 $1.00

LOVE: A Book of Quotations, Herb Galewitz (ed.). 64pp. 40004-2 $1.00

EVANGELINE AND OTHER POEMS, Henry Wadsworth Longfellow. 64pp. 28255-4 $1.00

CIVIL WAR POETRY AND PROSE, Walt Whitman. 96pp. 28507-3 $1.00

SELECTED POEMS, Walt Whitman. 128pp. 26878-0 $1.00

THE BALLAD OF READING GAOL AND OTHER POEMS, Oscar Wilde. 64pp. 27072-6 $1.00

FAVORITE POEMS, William Wordsworth. 80pp. 27073-4 $1.00

WORLD WAR ONE BRITISH POETS: Brooke, Owen, Sassoon, Rosenberg and Others, Candace Ward (ed.). (Available in U.S. only) 29568-0 $1.00

THE CAVALIER POETS: An Anthology, Thomas Crofts (ed.). 80pp. 28766-1 $1.00

ENGLISH ROMANTIC POETRY: An Anthology, Stanley Appelbaum (ed.). 256pp. 29282-7 $2.00

EARLY POEMS, William Butler Yeats. 128pp. 27808-5 $1.50

"EASTER, 1916" AND OTHER POEMS, William Butler Yeats. 80pp. (Available in U.S. only) 29771-3 $1.00

DOVER·THRIFT·EDITIONS

FICTION

FLATLAND: A ROMANCE OF MANY DIMENSIONS, Edwin A. Abbott. 96pp. 27263-X $1.00

PERSUASION, Jane Austen. 224pp. 29555-9 $2.00

PRIDE AND PREJUDICE, Jane Austen. 272pp. 28473-5 $2.00

SENSE AND SENSIBILITY, Jane Austen. 272pp. 29049-2 $2.00

WUTHERING HEIGHTS, Emily Brontë. 256pp. 29256-8 $2.00

BEOWULF, Beowulf (trans. by R. K. Gordon). 64pp. 27264-8 $1.00

CIVIL WAR STORIES, Ambrose Bierce. 128pp. 28038-1 $1.00

THE AUTOBIOGRAPHY OF AN EX-COLORED MAN, James Weldon Johnson. 112pp. 28512-X $1.00

TARZAN OF THE APES, Edgar Rice Burroughs. 224pp. (Available in U.S. only) 29570-2 $2.00

ALICE'S ADVENTURES IN WONDERLAND, Lewis Carroll. 96pp. 27543-4 $1.00

O PIONEERS!, Willa Cather. 128pp. 27785-2 $1.00

MY ÁNTONIA, Willa Cather. 176pp. 28240-6 $2.00

PAUL'S CASE AND OTHER STORIES, Willa Cather. 64pp. 29057-3 $1.00

IN A GERMAN PENSION: 13 Stories, Katherine Mansfield. 112pp. 28719-X $1.50

THE STORY OF AN AFRICAN FARM, Olive Schreiner. 256pp. 40165-0 $2.00

"THE YELLOW WALLPAPER" AND OTHER STORIES, Charlotte Perkins Gilman. 80pp. 29857-4 $1.00

HERLAND, Charlotte Perkins Gilman. 128pp. 40429-3 $1.50

FIVE GREAT SHORT STORIES, Anton Chekhov. 96pp. 26463-7 $1.00

"THE FIDDLER OF THE REELS" AND OTHER SHORT STORIES, Thomas Hardy. 80pp. 29960-0 $1.50

FAVORITE FATHER BROWN STORIES, G. K. Chesterton. 96pp. 27545-0 $1.00

THE WARDEN, Anthony Trollope. 176pp. 40076-X $2.00

THE COUNTRY OF THE POINTED FIRS, Sarah Orne Jewett. 96pp. 28196-5 $1.00

GREAT SHORT STORIES BY AMERICAN WOMEN, Candace Ward (ed.). 192pp. 28776-9 $2.00

SHORT STORIES, Louisa May Alcott. 64pp. 29063-8 $1.00

THE AWAKENING, Kate Chopin. 128pp. 27786-0 $1.00

A PAIR OF SILK STOCKINGS AND OTHER STORIES, Kate Chopin. 64pp. 29264-9 $1.00

THE REVOLT OF "MOTHER" AND OTHER STORIES, Mary E. Wilkins Freeman. 128pp. 40428-5 $1.50

HEART OF DARKNESS, Joseph Conrad. 80pp. 26464-5 $1.00

THE SECRET SHARER AND OTHER STORIES, Joseph Conrad. 128pp. 27546-9 $1.00

THE "LITTLE REGIMENT" AND OTHER CIVIL WAR STORIES, Stephen Crane. 80pp. 29557-5 $1.00

THE OPEN BOAT AND OTHER STORIES, Stephen Crane. 128pp. 27547-7 $1.50

THE RED BADGE OF COURAGE, Stephen Crane. 112pp. 26465-3 $1.00

A CHRISTMAS CAROL, Charles Dickens. 80pp. 26865-9 $1.00

THE CRICKET ON THE HEARTH AND OTHER CHRISTMAS STORIES, Charles Dickens. 128pp. 28039-X $1.00

THE DOUBLE, Fyodor Dostoyevsky. 128pp. 29572-9 $1.50

NOTES FROM THE UNDERGROUND, Fyodor Dostoyevsky. 96pp. 27053-X $1.00

THE GAMBLER, Fyodor Dostoyevsky. 112pp. 29081-6 $1.50

THE ADVENTURE OF THE DANCING MEN AND OTHER STORIES, Sir Arthur Conan Doyle. 80pp. 29558-3 $1.00

THE HOUND OF THE BASKERVILLES, Arthur Conan Doyle. 128pp. 28214-7 $1.00

SIX GREAT SHERLOCK HOLMES STORIES, Sir Arthur Conan Doyle. 112pp. 27055-6 $1.00

SILAS MARNER, George Eliot. 160pp. 29246-0 $1.50

DOVER · THRIFT · EDITIONS

FICTION

MADAME BOVARY, Gustave Flaubert. 256pp. 29257-6 $2.00

WHERE ANGELS FEAR TO TREAD, E. M. Forster. 128pp. (Available in U.S. only) 27791-7 $1.50

A ROOM WITH A VIEW, E. M. Forster. 176pp. (Available in U.S. only) 28467-0 $2.00

THE OVERCOAT AND OTHER STORIES, Nikolai Gogol. 112pp. 27057-2 $1.50

GREAT GHOST STORIES, John Grafton (ed.). 112pp. 27270-2 $1.00

"THE MOONLIT ROAD" AND OTHER GHOST AND HORROR STORIES, Ambrose Bierce (John Grafton, ed.) 96pp. 40056-5 $1.00

THE MABINOGION, Lady Charlotte E. Guest. 192pp. 29541-9 $2.00

WINESBURG, OHIO, Sherwood Anderson. 160pp. 28269-4 $2.00

THE LUCK OF ROARING CAMP AND OTHER STORIES, Bret Harte. 96pp. 27271-0 $1.00

THIS SIDE OF PARADISE, F. Scott Fitzgerald. 208pp. 28999-0 $2.00

"THE DIAMOND AS BIG AS THE RITZ" AND OTHER STORIES, F. Scott Fitzgerald. 29991-0 $2.00

THE SCARLET LETTER, Nathaniel Hawthorne. 192pp. 28048-9 $2.00

YOUNG GOODMAN BROWN AND OTHER STORIES, Nathaniel Hawthorne. 128pp. 27060-2 $1.00

THE GIFT OF THE MAGI AND OTHER SHORT STORIES, O. Henry. 96pp. 27061-0 $1.00

THE NUTCRACKER AND THE GOLDEN POT, E. T. A. Hoffmann. 128pp. 27806-9 $1.00

THE BEAST IN THE JUNGLE AND OTHER STORIES, Henry James. 128pp. 27552-3 $1.00

DAISY MILLER, Henry James. 64pp. 28773-4 $1.00

WASHINGTON SQUARE, Henry James. 176pp. 40431-5 $2.00

THE TURN OF THE SCREW, Henry James. 96pp. 26684-2 $1.00

DUBLINERS, James Joyce. 160pp. 26870-5 $1.00

A PORTRAIT OF THE ARTIST AS A YOUNG MAN, James Joyce. 192pp. 28050-0 $2.00

DEATH IN VENICE, Thomas Mann. 96pp. (Available in U.S. only) 28714-9 $1.00

THE METAMORPHOSIS AND OTHER STORIES, Franz Kafka. 96pp. 29030-1 $1.50

THE MAN WHO WOULD BE KING AND OTHER STORIES, Rudyard Kipling. 128pp. 28051-9 $1.50

SREDNI VASHTAR AND OTHER STORIES, Saki (H. H. Munro). 96pp. 28521-9 $1.00

THE OIL JAR AND OTHER STORIES, Luigi Pirandello. 96pp. 28459-X $1.00

SELECTED SHORT STORIES, D. H. Lawrence. 128pp. 27794-1 $1.00

GREEN TEA AND OTHER GHOST STORIES, J. Sheridan LeFanu. 96pp. 27795-X $1.00

SHORT STORIES, Theodore Dreiser. 112pp. 28215-5 $1.50

THE CALL OF THE WILD, Jack London. 64pp. 26472-6 $1.00

FIVE GREAT SHORT STORIES, Jack London. 96pp. 27063-7 $1.00

WHITE FANG, Jack London. 160pp. 26968-X $1.00

THE NECKLACE AND OTHER SHORT STORIES, Guy de Maupassant. 128pp. 27064-5 $1.00

BARTLEBY AND BENITO CERENO, Herman Melville. 112pp. 26473-4 $1.00

THE GOLD-BUG AND OTHER TALES, Edgar Allan Poe. 128pp. 26875-6 $1.00

TALES OF TERROR AND DETECTION, Edgar Allan Poe. 96pp. 28744-0 $1.00

DETECTION BY GASLIGHT, Douglas G. Greene (ed.). 272pp. 29928-7 $2.00

THE THIRTY-NINE STEPS, John Buchan. 96pp. 28201-5 $1.50

THE QUEEN OF SPADES AND OTHER STORIES, Alexander Pushkin. 128pp. 28054-3 $1.50

FIRST LOVE AND DIARY OF A SUPERFLUOUS MAN, Ivan Turgenev. 96pp. 28775-0 $1.50

FATHERS AND SONS, Ivan Turgenev. 176pp. 40073-5 $2.00

FRANKENSTEIN, Mary Shelley. 176pp. 28211-2 $1.00

THREE LIVES, Gertrude Stein. 176pp. (Available in U.S. only) 28059-4 $2.00